PRONUNCIATION GUIDE CHARTS & PICTURES

YOU TOO CAN SPEAK ENGLISH

SDA BOOKS

PRONUNCIATION GUIDE

YOU TOO CAN SPEAK ENGLISH

Table of Contents

Level · 5 145

Level · 6 169

Preface

Purpose

Clear pronunciation is required for clear communication, while poor pronunciation produces only confusion. That is, excellent grammar is wasted if the spoken words cannot be understood. This pronunciation guide is designed to improve students' pronunciation, intonation and connected speech so that they can speak clearly and confidently in English.

Description

To achieve its purpose, this guide focuses on the pronunciation challenges common among Koreans. In addition, to increase effectiveness and practicality, the vocabulary has been drawn from the most frequently used words in the English language.

Throughout the six levels of this book, students will practice daily the pronunciation of words and sentences. Levels 1 - 4 strongly focus on pronunciation while practicing intonation through repeated sentences. Levels 5 - 6 reinforce pronunciation skills while emphasizing intonation and connected speech through short journal entries.

Within each lesson, the letters in **bold type** signify the syllable of the word most stressed. Please note that syllables are divided differently for learning pronunciation than they are for learning to read. Both the pronunciation and syllable stress are taken from the Merriam-Webster online dictionary.

Study Tips

Before class, students should listen to the CD to hear instructions in Korean for how to form each sound. After class, they should also review with the CD and choose one or two target words to practice often in daily conversation.

Classroom Usage

In Levels 1 - 4, students will first practice how to form the daily target sound. Then they will listen and repeat as the teacher reads the words and the sentences listed.

In Levels 5 - 6, students will first practice the formation of the daily target sounds. Then they will listen as the teacher reads the passage. As they listen, students should make note of intonation, flow and any difficult words. Then they will listen and repeat as the teacher reads sentence by sentence.

You Too Can
Speak English

Chart of Phonetic Symbols

From the American Phonetic Alphabet

Consonants			
/b/	**b**at	/p/	**p**lay
/č/	**ch**ild	/r/	**r**an
/d/	**d**id	/s/	**s**it
/f/	**f**riend	/š/	**sh**ort
/g/	**g**et	/t/	**t**ime
/j/	**j**oy	/θ/	**th**in
/k/	**k**eep	/ð/	**th**em
/l/	**l**ady	/v/	**v**ery
/m/	**m**any	/w/	**w**in
/n/	**n**ot	/z/	**z**oo
/ŋ/	thi**ng**	/ž/	u**s**ually

Vowels			
/æ/	**a**dd	/ɔ/	**ou**ght
/e/	**a**te	/o/	**o**cean
/ɛ/	**e**nd	/oy/	t**oy**
/i/	**ea**t	/aw/	**ou**t
/I/	**i**t	/ə/	**u**s
/ay/	**eye**	/U/	l**oo**k
/a/	**o**pera	/u/	f**oo**d

LEVEL 1

/p/ party

● Day 1

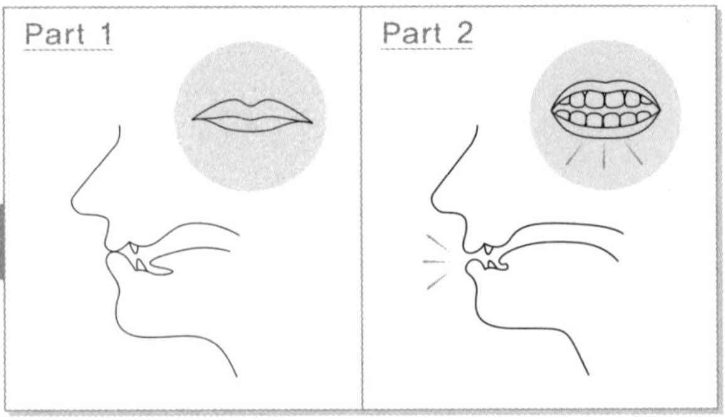

To make the /p/ sound, press your lips together. Then release your lips with a puff of air. Do not vibrate your vocal cords.

Words

INITIAL	MEDIAL	FINAL
party	ex**per**ience	camp
please	ex**am**ple	help
person	**o**pen	jump
plan	**o**pposite	rope
Peter	sur**prise**	trip

Sentences

1. Please ask that person to help us.
2. What's the opposite of *open*?
3. Did you ever jump rope or hula-hoop as a kid?
4. I'm planning a surprise party for Peter.
5. The camping trip was a pleasant experience.

/p/ people

● Day 2

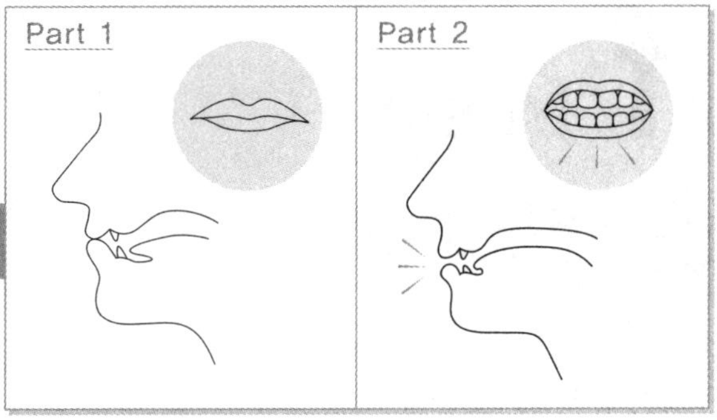

To make the /p/ sound, press your lips together. Then release your lips with a puff of air. Do not vibrate your vocal cords.

Words	INITIAL	MEDIAL	FINAL
	people	im**por**tant	up
	part	**pa**per	group
	place	per**haps**	keep
	put	space	top
	probably	u**pon**	deep

Sentences

1. Place the important papers on that pile.
2. They have space in their group for five people.
3. She probably put your pen on your desk.
4. Perhaps we'll be apart forever.
5. Patrick keeps his pillows on the top shelf.

/f/ friend

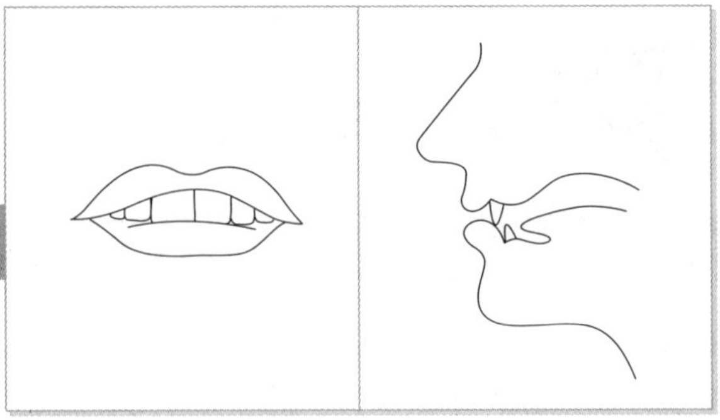

● Day 1

To make the /f/ sound, gently touch the inside of your lower lip with your teeth. Force air through your teeth. Your lower lip should not move when the air is forced out. Do not vibrate your vocal cords.

Words

INITIAL	MEDIAL	FINAL
friend	a**fraid**	life
floor	**di**fficult	half
fourth	**em**phasis	my**self**
fruit	**o**ffice	laugh
phrase	**care**fully	**Jo**seph

Sentences

1. I'm not afraid to be myself with Tiffany.
2. Sometimes it's difficult to laugh at life.
3. My friend ate half of my fruit.
4. Joseph's office is on the fourth floor.
5. Please read each phrase carefully.

/f/ first

● Day 2

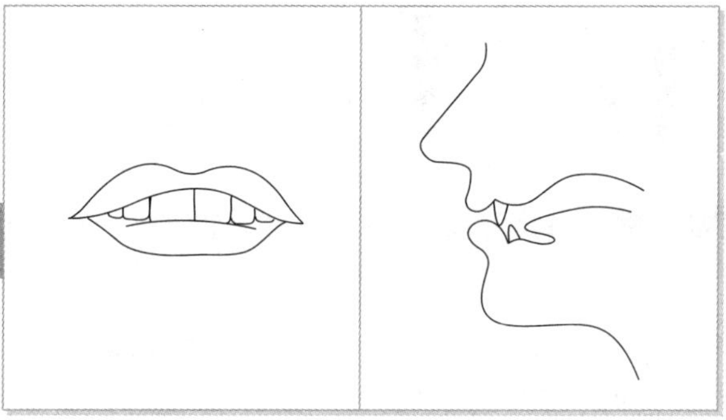

To make the /f/ sound, gently touch the inside of your lower lip with your teeth. Force air through your teeth. Your lower lip should not move when the air is forced out. Do not vibrate your vocal cords.

Words

INITIAL	MEDIAL	FINAL
first	left	if
from	be**fore**	safe
folks	**a**fter	him**self**
free	**sur**face	e**nough**
phone	phi**lo**sophy	**pho**tograph

Sentences

1. Should we meet before or after breakfast?
2. You can call him from my cell phone if you want to.
3. Frank never has enough free time.
4. It's not safe to walk on a slippery surface.
5. Some folks confuse their left foot with their right foot.

/p/ & /f/ pig-fig

Review

Practice distinguishing between the /p/ and /f/ sounds. Remember that the /p/ sound is formed by a burst of air from your lips while the /f/ sound is formed using your upper teeth and lower lip.

Words	INITIAL	MEDIAL	FINAL
	pig - fig	**co**py - **co**ffee	cup - cuff
	pair - fair	shipped - shift	wipe - wife
	peer - fear	de**pend** - de**fend**	pup - puff
	past - fast	**di**pper - **di**ffer	clip - cliff
	pat - fat	**su**pper - **su**ffer	cheap - chief

Sentences

1. The pair of pigs won first prize at the fair.
2. I left my hair clip on the front porch.
3. Fred spilled coffee on the copy machine.
4. Finish your supper as fast as you can.
5. My wife is the chief executive officer of Air France.

/b/ be

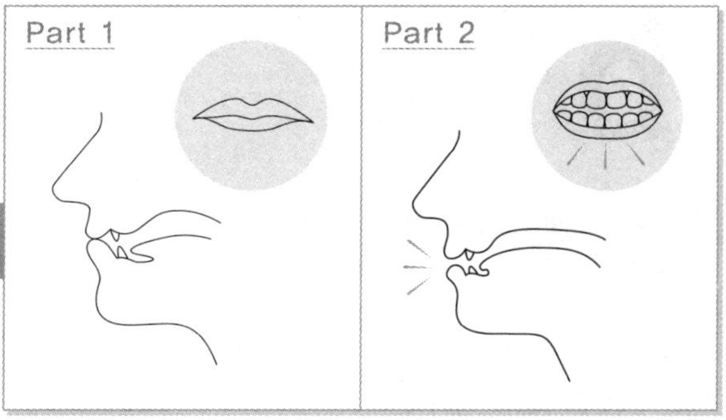

● Day 1

To make the /b/ sound, form the shape of the /p/ sound with your mouth. Make the same sound, this time vibrating your vocal cords.

Words

INITIAL	MEDIAL	FINAL
be	a**bove**	job
buy	**trou**ble	tube
blow	**sub**ject	verb
better	**sym**bol	de**scribe**
be**hind**	**dou**ble	Bob

Sentences

1. I'd better buy a tube of toothpaste.
2. Describe your job for us, Bob.
3. I'll be in trouble if I get behind in Biology.
4. I'm better than my brother in most subjects.
5. What does that big symbol above the door mean?

/b/ bank

● Day 2

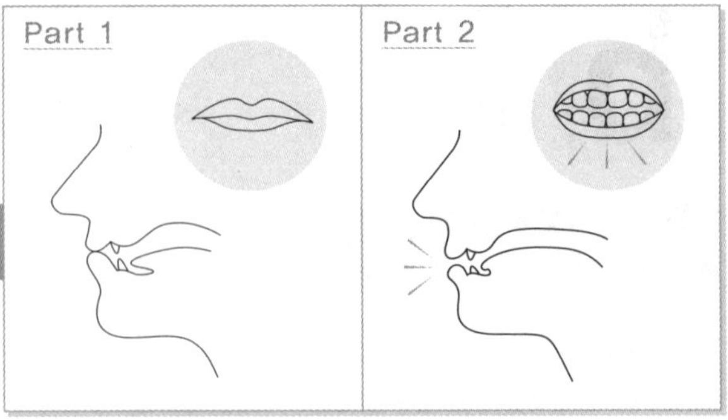

To make the /b/ sound, form the shape of the /p/ sound with your mouth. Make the same sound, this time vibrating your vocal cords.

Words

INITIAL	MEDIAL	FINAL
bank	**pu**blic	globe
basic	**ca**bin	tribe
beat	**eve**rybody	rob
bone	**mem**ber	club
bread	**base**ball	pub

Sentences

1. Bill is a member of the badminton club.
2. My favorite baseball team beat the Boston Red Sox.
3. Beth went to a public bathhouse yesterday.
4. The bank was robbed by two brothers.
5. I bought bread and peanut butter for breakfast.

/V/ very

● Day 1

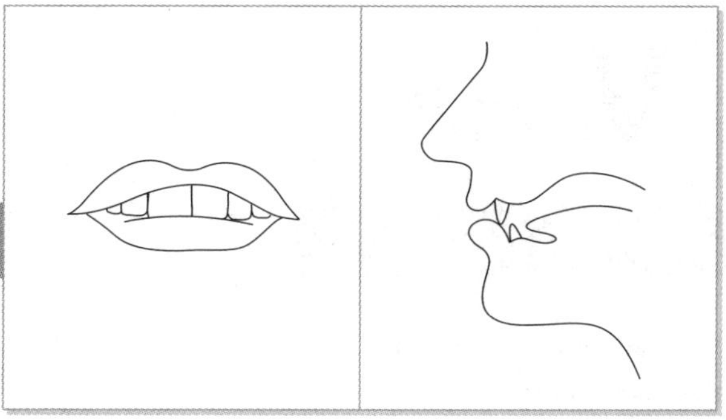

To make the /v/ sound, form the shape of the /f/ sound with your mouth. Make the same sound, this time vibrating your vocal cords.

Words

INITIAL	MEDIAL	FINAL
very	**e**ven	give
voice	**ne**ver	have
various	**ev**ery	five
value	**o**ver	move
valley	**gi**ven	leave

Sentences

1. What is the value of land in the river valley?
2. If you give me five minutes, I'll have the project finished.
3. I've been very lonely since my best friend moved away.
4. Valerie has never visited Vermont.
5. The bus is leaving for Vancouver even as we speak.

/V/ visit

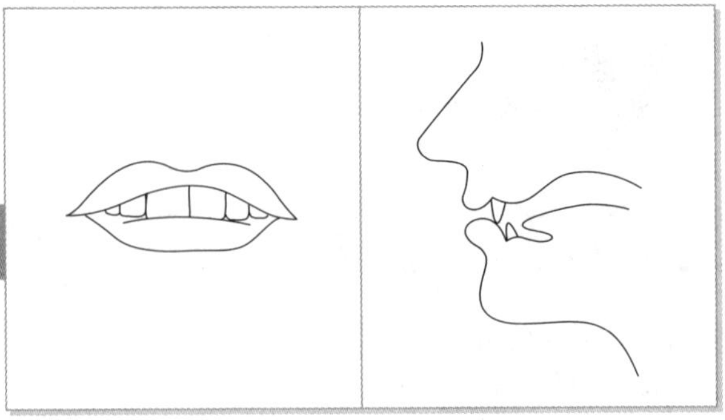

● Day 2

To make the /v/ sound, form the shape of the /f/ sound with your mouth. Make the same sound, this time vibrating your vocal cords.

Words

INITIAL	MEDIAL	FINAL
visit	**li**ving	I've
village	**seve**ral	love
va**ri**ety	**eve**ryone	wave
valuable	**ha**ving	live
vast	**e**ver	of

Sentences

1. She's been living in Jacksonville for five years.
2. I've been trying to tell you every day that I love you.
3. Everyone, please wave for the video!
4. I've been having this problem for several days.
5. Canada's vast forests provide many valuable resources.

/b/ & /v/ best-vest

Review

Practice distinguishing between the /b/ and /v/ sounds. Remember that the /b/ sound is formed by a burst of air from your lips while the /v/ sound is formed using your upper teeth and lower lip.

Words

INITIAL	MEDIAL	FINAL
best - vest	**re**bel - **re**vel	curb - curve
ban - van	lobes - loaves	strobe - strove
bent - vent	**mar**ble - **mar**vel	dub - dove
bet - vet	**cu**pboard - **co**vered	swab - suave
bow - vow	TB - TV	Gabe - gave

Sentences

1. She bent over to pick up the marbles.
2. It is best to vent any frustrations you have.
3. I bet I can beat you to that curve in the road.
4. We should bow and introduce ourselves to the bride's parents.
5. The man carried a heavy book in his vest pocket.

/l/ like

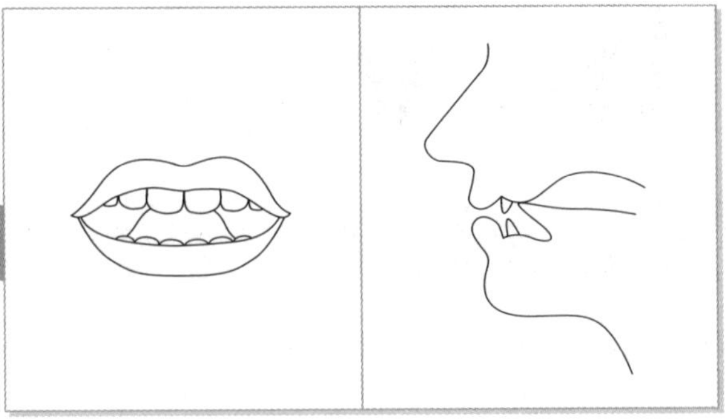

● Day 1

To form the /l/ sound, press the tip of your tongue against the top of your mouth along the ridge that is behind your upper front teeth. The sides of your tongue should not be touching anything. Vibrate your vocal cords and give your tongue a little extra push against the top of your mouth.

Words

INITIAL	MEDIAL	FINAL
like	**fam**ily	will
large	a**long**	fell
look	be**low**	**bi**cycle
long	old	wheel
letter	he**llo**	tell

Sentences

1. They look like they're in love.
2. Will you walk with me along the river?
3. Tell your family hello for me.
4. How long should this letter to Michael be?
5. The wheel fell off the bicycle.

/l/ last

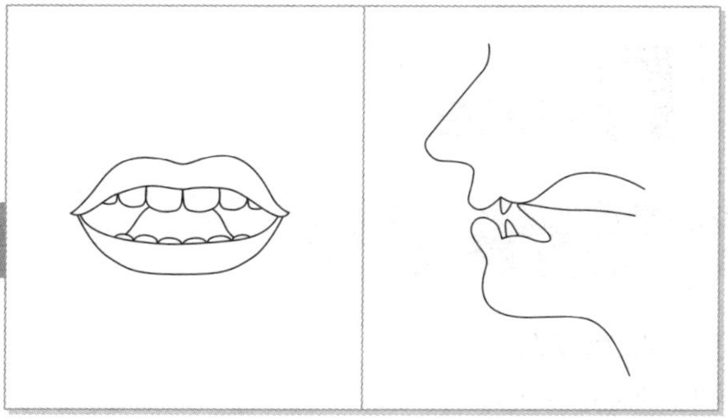

Day 2

To form the /l/ sound, press the tip of your tongue against the top of your mouth along the ridge that is behind your upper front teeth. The sides of your tongue should not be touching anything. Vibrate your vocal cords and give your tongue a little extra push against the top of your mouth.

Words

INITIAL	MEDIAL	FINAL
last	**al**so	small
line	**on**ly	still
land	world	well
later	**al**most	while
learn	black	all

Sentences

1. It's a small world after all.
2. The last lines of the dialogue are difficult to learn.
3. It's almost time for the plane to land.
4. I still don't feel well.
5. Can we play Monopoly later?

/r/ race

● Day 1

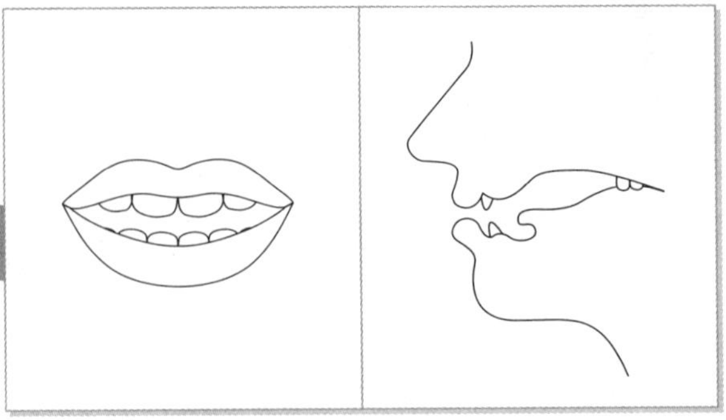

To make the /r/ sound, press the sides of your tongue against the inside of your upper back molar teeth. The rest of your tongue should not be touching anything. Vibrate your vocal cords.

Words	INITIAL	MEDIAL	FINAL
	race	a**round**	**doc**tor
	ran	great	a**no**ther
	room	three	**su**mmer
	ready	word	your
	write	**par**agraph	chair

Sentences

1. Write a three-paragraph essay about your summer.
2. Are you ready for another term?
3. The boy sat in a chair in the doctor's waiting room.
4. Ryan ran the race and came in third.
5. I had a great time traveling around Europe.

/r/ red

● Day 2

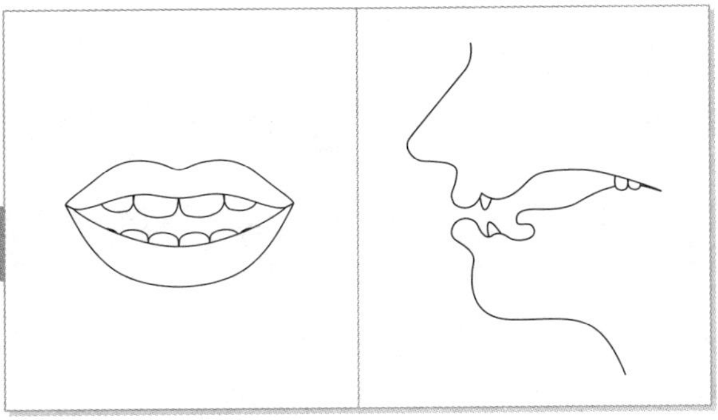

To make the /r/ sound, press the sides of your tongue against the inside of your upper back molar teeth. The rest of your tongue should not be touching anything. Vibrate your vocal cords.

Words	INITIAL	MEDIAL	FINAL
	red	through	**sis**ter
	radio	a**rrive**	her
	rest	work	are
	re**mem**ber	**ear**ly	for
	wrong	**mor**ning	here

Sentences

1. What's wrong with your sister?
2. I'll arrive early tomorrow morning.
3. Do you have a radio in your bedroom?
4. She drove her car through a red light.
5. Let's rest here for three or four minutes.

/l/ & /r/ light-right

Review

Practice distinguishing between the /l/ and /r/ sounds. Remember that the /l/ sound is formed using the tip of your tongue while the /r/ sound is formed using the sides of your tongue.

Words

INITIAL	MEDIAL	FINAL
light - right	cloud - crowd	mole - more
lead - read	co**ll**ect - co**rr**ect	roll - roar
lied - ride	cold - cord	stole - store
liver - **ri**ver	fly - fry	**for**mal - **for**mer
low - row	glass - grass	**tow**el - **tow**er

Sentences

1. Please fry the egg a little longer.
2. I'll go to the store when it's less crowded.
3. I often catch colds when the weather gets colder.
4. Leave the porch light on at night.
5. There was a large fire near the river.

/t/ time

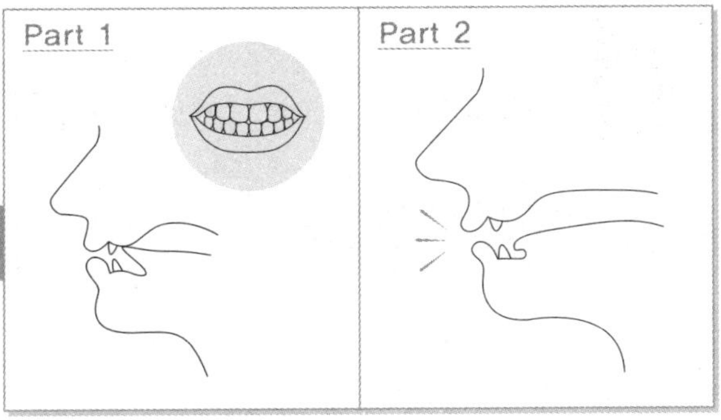

To make the /t/ sound, press the tip of your tongue against the ridge that is behind your upper front teeth. Then, without vibrating your vocal cords, release your tongue with a puff of air.

Words

INITIAL	MEDIAL	FINAL
time	**in**to	a**bout**
take	it's	at
too	**pre**tty	but
to**ge**ther	**ci**ty	don't
tree	**coun**try	get

Sentences

1. Can I take these with me into the store?
2. What happened to you this time?
3. It's nice to see you too.
4. The country was in pretty bad shape after the tornado.
5. How do I get to City Hall?

/d/ day

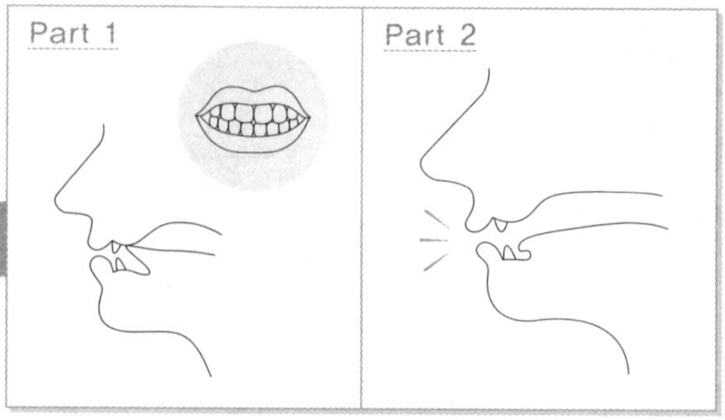

To make the /d/ sound, form the shape of the /t/ sound with your mouth. Make the same sound, this time vibrating your vocal cords.

Words	INITIAL	MEDIAL	FINAL
	day	**hun**dred	and
	do	**su**ddenly	could
	does	**cou**ldn't	end
	draw	**un**der	good
	did	**mo**dern	found

Sentences

1. I've drawn hundreds of pictures for my grandfather.
2. He found the dog hiding under the bed.
3. The food was good, but I couldn't finish it.
4. What does the word *modern* mean?
5. We suddenly decided to do something different.

/t/ & /d/ town-down

Review

Practice distinguishing between the /t/ and /d/ sounds. Remember that the formation of the mouth is the same for these two sounds. /t/ is the sound formed without vibrating your vocal cords. /d/ is the sound formed while vibrating your vocal cords.

Words

INITIAL	MEDIAL	FINAL
town - down	**cen**ter - **sen**der	a**bort** - a**board**
tot - dot	**hur**ting - **her**ding	beat - bead
train - drain	**li**ter - **lea**der	cart - card
touch - Dutch	**wri**ter - **ri**der	bit - bid
tan - Dan	**ea**ten - **E**den	boat - bode

Sentences

1. I've received a lot of email from random senders.
2. Did you beat Dan at *yut?*
3. Beads of sweat dripped down the man's face.
4. Have you eaten dinner yet?
5. I'm taking a train to Detroit.

-ed endings

●Day 1

The -ed ending can be pronounced in three ways.

- It can be pronounced as /t/. No vowel sound is added before the /t/. Once your tongue is released, quickly stop the air from flowing through your open mouth.
- It can also be pronounced as /d/. No vowel sound is added before the /d/. Once your tongue is released, quickly stop the air from flowing through your open mouth.
- It can also be an unstressed final syllable pronounced as /Id/. Your lips should be loosely parted, while the tongue is relaxed, forming the /I/ sound. Vibrate your vocal cords and immediately push the tip of your tongue against the top of your mouth, forming the /d/ sound.

Words

FINAL /t/	FINAL /d/	FINAL /Id/
stopped	joined	**nee**ded
dropped	**carr**ied	u**ni**ted
wished	**ha**ppened	re**la**ted
a**ttached**	tried	ex**ci**ted
slipped	con**tin**ued	**prin**ted

Sentences

1. I stopped buying gas because I no longer needed it.
2. I tried to explain what had happened, but no one listened.
3. How many countries have joined the United Nations?
4. I was very excited when I dropped my calculus class.
5. After I slipped and fell, he carried me home.

-ed endings

● Day 2

The -ed ending can be pronounced in three ways.

- It can be pronounced as /t/. No vowel sound is added before the /t/. Once your tongue is released, quickly stop the air from flowing through your open mouth.
- It can also be pronounced as /d/. No vowel sound is added before the /d/. Once your tongue is released, quickly stop the air from flowing through your open mouth.
- It can also be an unstressed final syllable pronounced as /Id/. Your lips should be loosely parted, while the tongue is relaxed, forming the /I/ sound. Vibrate your vocal cords and immediately push the tip of your tongue against the top of your mouth, forming the /d/ sound.

Words	FINAL /t/	FINAL /d/	FINAL /Id/
	a**nnounced**	re**plied**	in**ven**ted
	intro**duced**	**hurr**ied	co**nnec**ted
	promised	dried	**hea**ded
	wrapped	**stu**died	su**rroun**ded
	stepped	com**posed**	**li**mited

Sentences

1. She replied quickly to my letter, just like she had promised.
2. They announced their engagement to a limited number of people.
3. He was surrounded by people waiting to be introduced.
4. She wished she would have studied more.
5. I missed the train even though I had hurried.

/θ/ thing

● Day 1

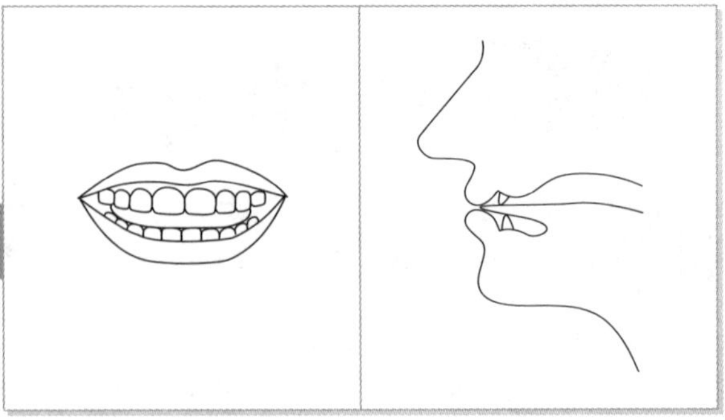

To make the /θ/ sound, put the tip of your tongue between your top and bottom front teeth. Let air escape around your tongue without vibrating your vocal cords.

Words	INITIAL	MEDIAL	FINAL
	thing	**au**thor	north
	thought	**some**thing	south
	think	**a**nything	both
	third	**no**thing	with
	thousand	wi**thout**	earth

Sentences

1. I think Thoreau was a great author.
2. A third of the earth's population lives without power.
3. I thought about going with them, but something came up.
4. She visited both North and South Korea.
5. Katherine couldn't understand anything without translation.

/θ/ thick

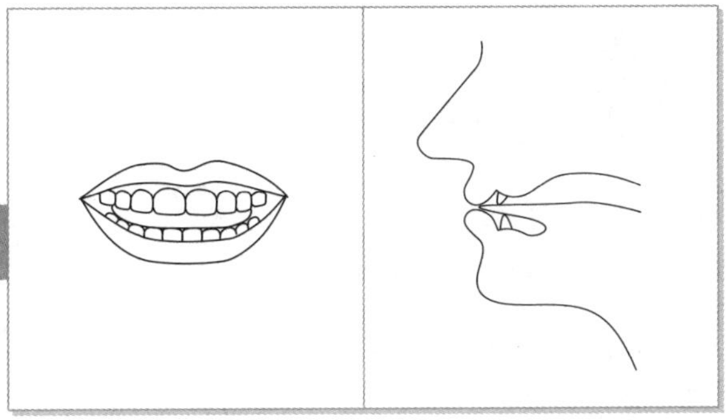

● Day 2

To make the /θ/ sound, put the tip of your tongue between your top and bottom front teeth. Let air escape around your tongue without vibrating your vocal cords.

Words

INITIAL	MEDIAL	FINAL
thick	**eve**rything	length
thin	wi**thin**	month
through**out**	**me**thod	death
threw	**birth**day	cloth
throw	mathe**ma**tics	forth

Sentences

1. I'll be with you through thick and thin.
2. We threw a birthday party for Elizabeth last month.
3. All throughout the world, people mourned General MacArthur's death.
4. His method of teaching mathematics is very thorough.
5. Theo can throw a football the length of the field.

/ð/ that

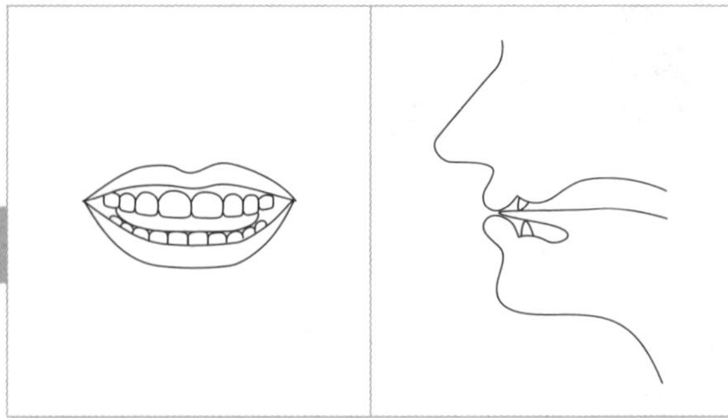

● Day 1

To make the /ð/ sound, form the shape of the /θ/ sound with your mouth. Make the same sound, this time vibrating your vocal cords.

Words	INITIAL	MEDIAL	FINAL
	that	**mo**ther	tithe
	there	**fa**ther	soothe
	than	**bro**ther	clothe
	they	**o**ther	bathe
	the	al**though**	breathe

Sentences

1. It's hard to breathe when I bathe in cold water.
2. The sound of the waves soothed my nerves.
3. There is a friend that sticks closer than a brother.
4. Feed and clothe the babies before they go to the doctor.
5. Does your brother live with your mother and father?

/ð/ them

● Day 2

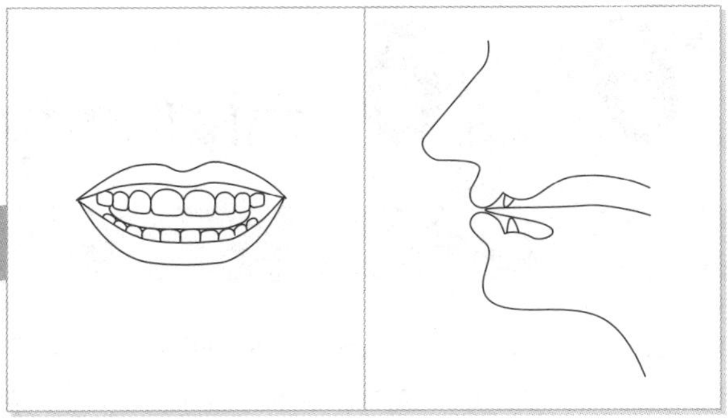

To make the /ð/ sound, form the shape of the /θ/ sound with your mouth. Make the same sound, this time vibrating your vocal cords.

Words	INITIAL	MEDIAL	FINAL
	them	**fur**ther	loathe
	them**selves**	**sou**thern	smooth
	then	**wea**ther	writhe
	these	**fea**thers	blithe
	this	**ra**ther	**sun**bathe

Sentences

1. This cold weather is terrible for sunbathing.
2. My home is in the southern part of the Netherlands.
3. I hope the students enjoy my lectures rather than loathe them.
4. I patted the bird's smooth feathers.
5. They couldn't convince themselves to go any further.

/θ/ & /ð/ thigh-thy

● Review

Practice distinguishing between the /θ/ and /ð/ sounds. Remember that the formation of the mouth is the same for these two sounds. /θ/ is the sound formed without vibrating your vocal cords. /ð/ is the sound formed while vibrating your vocal cords.

Words	INITIAL	MEDIAL	FINAL
	thigh - thy	**e**ther - **ei**ther	teeth - teethe
	thistle - **thi**s'll		mouth - mouth
			sheath - sheathe
			wreath - wreathe

Sentences

1. Babies get new teeth when they teethe.
2. I think this'll hurt your mouth a little.
3. Mouth all three of the words carefully.
4. I hit my thigh on the edge of the desk.
5. I don't like thorns, and I don't like thistles either.

/S/ sea

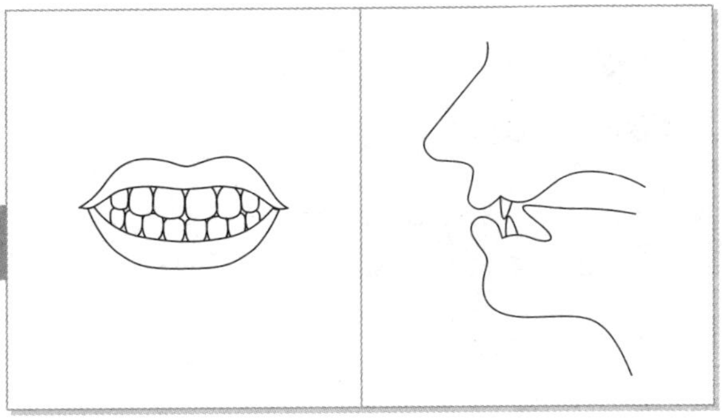

To make the /s/ sound, bite your teeth together gently. Raise the tip of your tongue toward the top of your mouth along the ridge that is behind your upper front teeth, but don't touch it. Let air hiss through that narrow opening without vibrating your vocal cords.

Words	INITIAL	MEDIAL	FINAL
	sea	**an**swer	class
	seen	de**cide**	di**scuss**
	sit	most	else
	since	must	face
	six	a**gainst**	yes

Sentences

1. What else do we need to discuss before Sunday?
2. Yes, I've decided to take the class.
3. He was sitting quietly with a smile on his face.
4. I am sometimes slow to answer.
5. I haven't seen the sea since I was a child.

/z/ zero

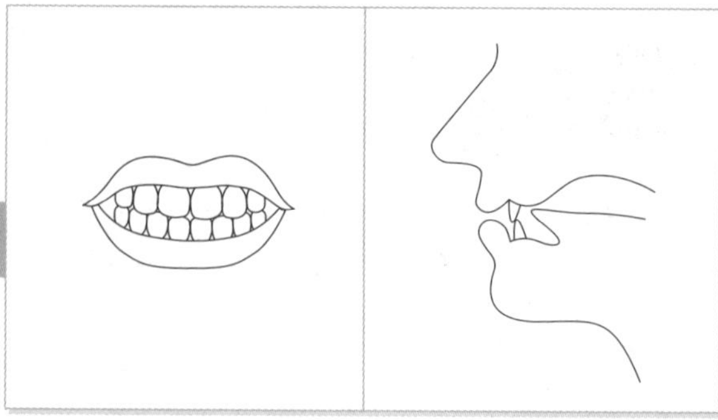

To make the /z/ sound, form the shape of the /s/ sound with your mouth. Make the same sound, this time vibrating your vocal cords.

Words

INITIAL	MEDIAL	FINAL
zero	**de**sert	his
zones	**u**sing	as
Zen	**bu**sy	be**cause**
Zealand	**mu**sic	is
Zambia	**ea**sy	has

Sentences

1. His home is in the desert.
2. Traveling across half a dozen time zones is not easy.
3. Nowadays, I'm too busy to listen to music.
4. She bought a Bible because she was interested in Jesus.
5. New Zealand has twice as many cats as dogs.

/S/ & /Z/ sip-zip

Review

Practice distinguishing between the /s/ and /z/ sounds. Remember that the formation of the mouth is the same for these two sounds. /s/ is the sound formed without vibrating your vocal cords. /z/ is the sound formed while vibrating your vocal cords.

Words

INITIAL	MEDIAL	FINAL
sip - zip	**mu**scle - **mu**zzle	place - plays
sink - zinc	**fa**cing - **pha**sing	piece - peas
sewn - zone	**ra**cer - **ra**zor	ice - eyes
seal - zeal	**la**cy - **la**zy	trace - trays
sue - zoo	**fu**ssy - **fu**zzy	fierce - fears

Sentences

1. I had to sit down and let the news sink in.
2. Isn't this a wonderful place?
3. When smoke gets in my eyes, it makes everything seem fuzzy.
4. The report received fierce criticism.
5. What fears are stopping you from achieving your goals?

-S endings

● Day 1

The -s ending can be pronounced in three ways.

- It can be pronounced as /s/. No vowel sound is added before the /s/. Before you release your tongue, quickly stop the air from flowing through your mouth.
- It can also be pronounced as /z/. No vowel sound is added before the /z/. Before you release your tongue, quickly stop the air from flowing through your mouth.
- It can also be an unstressed final syllable pronounced as /Iz/. Your lips should be loosely parted, while the tongue is relaxed, forming the /I/ sound. Vibrate your vocal cords and immediately raise the tip of your tongue toward the top of your mouth, forming the /z/ sound.

Words

FINAL /s/	FINAL /z/	FINAL /Iz/
lips	birds	**prac**tices
states	seems	ex**peri**ences
sets	means	**sta**ges
ants	po**ta**toes	**a**ges
parts	sides	ex**pen**ses

Sentences

1. He always seems to be able to spot interesting birds.
2. I had some crazy experiences while I was in the United States.
3. The whole equals the sum of its parts.
4. I can't sit still at meetings. I get ants in my pants.
5. Idaho grows more potatoes than any other state in the U.S.

-S endings

Day 2

The -s ending can be pronounced in three ways.

- It can be pronounced as /s/. No vowel sound is added before the /s/. Before you release your tongue, quickly stop the air from flowing through your mouth.
- It can also be pronounced as /z/. No vowel sound is added before the /z/. Before you release your tongue, quickly stop the air from flowing through your mouth.
- It can also be an unstressed final syllable pronounced as /Iz/. Your lips should be loosely parted, while the tongue is relaxed, forming the /I/ sound. Vibrate your vocal cords and immediately raise the tip of your tongue toward the top of your mouth, forming the /z/ sound.

Words

FINAL /s/	FINAL /z/	FINAL /Iz/
troops	needs	**lo**sses
thoughts	**sett**lers	**o**ffices
nuts	flies	**tax**es
plates	**min**erals	**char**ges
satellites	**par**ticles	**wa**ges

Sentences

1. We can get various vitamins and minerals from nuts.
2. The settlers suffered many losses when their homes were destroyed.
3. My thoughts are not your thoughts; my ways are not your ways.
4. The troops were assigned to wash the plates after breakfast.
5. She has taxes taken directly from her wages.

/p/ & /f/ pour-four

● Review

Practice distinguishing between the /p/ and /f/ sounds. Remember that the /p/ sound is formed by a burst of air from your lips while the /f/ sound is formed using your upper teeth and lower lip.

Words

INITIAL	MEDIAL	FINAL
pour - four	**chea**ply - **chie**fly	leap - leaf
paint - faint	de**pen**dent - de**fen**dant	clip - cliff
put - foot	sipped - sift	snip - sniff
pun - fun	laps - laughs	beep - beef
purr - fur	shipped - shift	cup - cuff

Sentences

1. Face painting is fun.
2. I found a way to travel to France cheaply.
3. The cat purred as I petted its fur.
4. Would you pour enough juice for four people?
5. Don't laugh if my pronunciation is bad.

/b/ & /v/ base-vase

Review

Practice distinguishing between the /b/ and /v/ sounds. Remember that the /b/ sound is formed by a burst of air from your lips while the /v/ sound is formed using your upper teeth and lower lip.

Words

INITIAL	MEDIAL	FINAL
base - vase	lobes - loaves	curb - curve
boat - vote	**sa**ber - **sa**vor	strobe - strove
ba**llet** - va**let**	**mar**ble - **mar**vel	dub - dove
beard - veered	**re**bel - **re**vel	swab - suave
bigger - **vi**gor	TB - TV	Gabe - gave

Sentences

1. Please bring me two loaves of bread.
2. Gabe savored the time his mother gave him.
3. The service on the cruise boat was marvelous.
4. It's been over three years since I've been to the ballet.
5. The building is covered with marble.

/l/ & /r/ late-rate

● Review

Practice distinguishing between the /l/ and /r/ sounds. Remember that the /l/ sound is formed using the tip of your tongue while the /r/ sound is formed using the sides of your tongue.

Words	INITIAL	MEDIAL	FINAL
	late - rate	**alive** - **arrive**	**for**mal - **for**mer
	load - road	blew - brew	stole - store
	lock - rock	play - pray	roll - roar
	led - red	**plea**sant - **pre**sent	**tow**el - **tow**er
	list - wrist	flight - fright	mole - more

Sentences

1. I really blew it.
2. What are the rates for your all-day tours?
3. I'll be working late tonight.
4. What time will your flight arrive?
5. I live just a kilometer or two down the road.

/θ/ & /s/ thick-sick

● Review

Practice distinguishing between the /θ/ and /s/ sounds. Remember that the /θ/ sound is formed with the tip of your tongue between your teeth while the /s/ sound is formed with the tip of your tongue near the ridge that is behind your upper front teeth.

Words

INITIAL	MEDIAL	FINAL
thick - sick	**youth**ful - **use**ful	worth - worse
thumb - some	**play**thing - **pla**cing	path - pass
think - sink	un**thin**kable - un**sin**kable	faith - face
thin - sin	frothed - frost	mouth - mouse
thimble - **cym**bal	**e**thics - **E**ssex	eighth - eights

Sentences

1. Her thick black hair fell across her face.
2. I think his website is worth checking out.
3. If things get any worse, you'll be on thin ice.
4. Please don't stick your thumb in your mouth.
5. Some people's ethics are affected by their faith.

/d/ & /z/ deal-zeal

Review

Practice distinguishing between the /d/ and /z/ sounds. Remember that the /d/ sound is formed by touching the ridge that is behind your upper front teeth with the tip of your tongue while the /z/ sound is formed by putting the tip of your tongue near that same ridge but not touching it.

Words

INITIAL	MEDIAL	FINAL
deal - zeal	**mu**ddle - **mu**zzle	card - cars
dipper - **zi**pper	**plea**ding - **plea**sing	**carr**ied - **carr**ies
do - zoo	**bu**dding - **bu**zzing	tried - tries
doom - zoom	**ri**dden - **ri**sen	dried - dries
den - Zen	**la**dy - **la**zy	**stu**died - **stu**dies

Sentences

1. We carried out the research in three distinct phases.
2. I bought two used cars from him the other day.
3. He carries on when others around him give up.
4. I've tried to start using more recycled products.
5. He dried his hands with a damp towel.

You Too Can Speak English
Pronunciation Guide

LEVEL 2

/p/ & /b/ pack-back

● Review

Practice distinguishing between the /p/ and /b/ sounds. Remember that the formation of the mouth is the same for these two sounds. /p/ is the sound formed without vibrating your vocal cords. /b/ is the sound formed while vibrating your vocal cords.

Words

INITIAL	MEDIAL	FINAL
pack - back	slaps - slabs	cap - cab
pear - bear	re**pel** - re**bel**	lap - lab
pace - base	**crum**ple - **crum**ble	mop - mob
pan - ban	**sim**ple - **cym**bal	tap - tab
Paul - ball	**sta**ple - **sta**ble	rip - rib

Sentences

1. I forgot my backpack in the taxicab.
2. Paul crumpled the letter into a ball.
3. The bear ripped the slab of meat apart.
4. I stapled the bibliography to the back of my report.
5. The police tried to stabilize the mob of protesters.

/f/ & /v/ fine-vine

Review

Practice distinguishing between the /f/ and /v/ sounds. Remember that the formation of the mouth is the same for these two sounds. /f/ is the sound formed without vibrating your vocal cords. /v/ is the sound formed while vibrating your vocal cords.

Words

INITIAL	MEDIAL	FINAL
fine - vine	**shu**ffle - **sho**vel	proof - prove
fewer - **view**er	re**fuse** - re**views**	shelf - shelve
failed - veiled	in**fest** - in**vest**	be**lief** - be**lieve**
ferry - **ver**y	**ri**fle - **ri**val	grief - grieve
fear - veer	**sur**face - **ser**vice	safe - save

Sentences

1. They refused to believe without proof.
2. Is it safer to invest my funds or to save them in the bank?
3. There is a fine view of the Statue of Liberty from the ferry.
4. The review failed to prove the play's value.
5. Learn from your failures. Don't grieve over them.

/l/ & /r/ lake-rake

● Review

Practice distinguishing between the /l/ and /r/ sounds. Remember that the /l/ sound is formed using the tip of your tongue while the /r/ sound is formed using the sides of your tongue.

Words

INITIAL	MEDIAL	FINAL
lake - rake	climb - crime	**for**mal - **for**mer
law - raw	flame - frame	**tow**el - **tow**er
lay - ray	glean - green	mole - more
lose - ruse	mis**led** - mis**read**	roll - roar
locket - **ro**cket	flank - Frank	stole - store

Sentences

1. Climbing the water tower is a crime.
2. My teacher never loses his patience with the class.
3. I had my picture taken in front of the Eiffel Tower.
4. Frank Miller and his brother opened a law firm.
5. I got raked over the coals for my serious error.

/θ/ & /ð/ thigh-thy

Review

Practice distinguishing between the /θ/ and /ð/ sounds. Remember that the formation of the mouth is the same for these two sounds. /θ/ is the sound formed without vibrating your vocal cords. /ð/ is the sound formed while vibrating your vocal cords.

Words

INITIAL	MEDIAL	FINAL
thigh - thy	**e**ther - **ei**ther	teeth - teethe
thistle - **thi**s'll		mouth - mouth
		sheath - sheathe
		wreath - wreathe

Sentences

1. Either wreath will look good on the front door.
2. This'll be their first visit to the theater.
3. A sheath holds a sword so it won't cut your thigh.
4. The teething baby has two teeth in its mouth.
5. They often use *thy* instead of *your* in the KJV Bible.

/S/ & /Z/ sap-zap

Review

Practice distinguishing between the /s/ and /z/ sounds. Remember that the formation of the mouth is the same for these two sounds. /s/ is the sound formed without vibrating your vocal cords. /z/ is the sound formed while vibrating your vocal cords.

Words

INITIAL	MEDIAL	FINAL
sap - zap	**loo**ser - **lo**ser	spice - spies
singer - **zing**er	**pre**cedent - **pre**sident	price - prize
sipping - **zi**pping	**fu**ssy - **fu**zzy	sauce - saws
seek - Zeke	**cea**sing - **sei**zing	bus - buzz
C - Z	de**vi**ces - de**vi**ses	dose - doze

Sentences

1. My clothes are looser because I've been losing weight.
2. She uses several spices in her prize-winning sauce.
3. The singer's house is only half an hour from here by bus.
4. The president was seized by his security guards.
5. The saws buzz without ceasing at the mill.

/s/ see

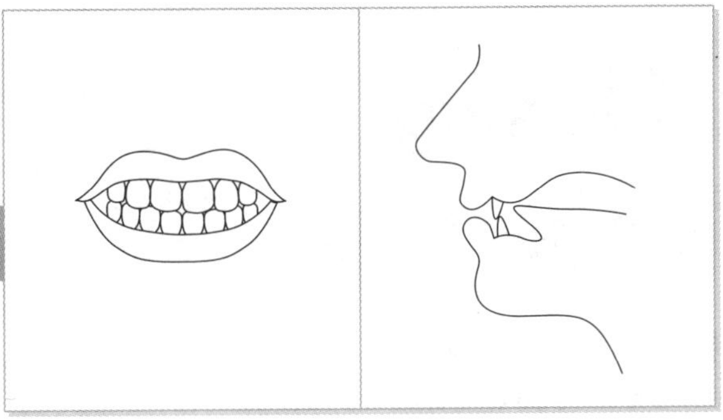

Review

Review the /s/ sound. Remember that the /s/ sound is made by biting your teeth together gently and raising the tip of your tongue toward the top of your mouth along the ridge that is behind your upper front teeth without touching it.

Words	INITIAL	MEDIAL	FINAL
	see	just	us
	seed	in**side**	house
	single	**dis**tance	a**cross**
	silver	Mr.	course
	similar	Mrs.	once

Sentences

1. A single seed can grow into a humongous tree.
2. Mr. Johnson will run the obstacle course only once.
3. From a distance, silver and gray look similar.
4. Mrs. Davis' house is just across the street.
5. Can you see us from inside your office?

/S/ sing

Review

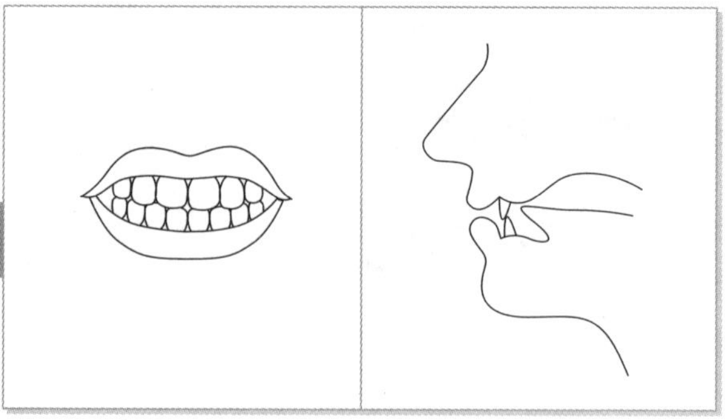

Review the /s/ sound. Remember that the /s/ sound is made by biting your teeth together gently and raising the tip of your tongue toward the top of your mouth along the ridge that is behind your upper front teeth without touching it.

Words

INITIAL	MEDIAL	FINAL
sing	in**stead**	let's
sitting	least	horse
simply	out**side**	**no**tice
seat	**po**ssible	**sen**tence
season	**sci**entist	Miss

Sentences

1. If possible, let's whisper instead of shouting.
2. It's beautiful outside when the seasons change.
3. I notice an empty seat next to Miss Nelson.
4. Write at least five sentences about horses.
5. The scientist presented a simple experiment to the students.

/š/ she

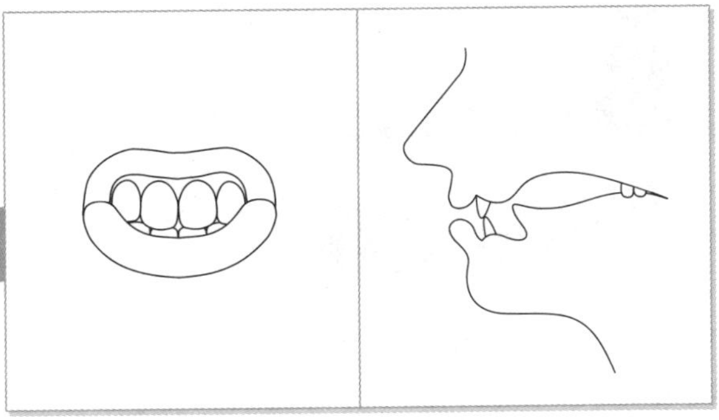

● Day 1

To make the /š/ sound, form the shape of the /s/ sound with your mouth. Then round your lips and pull the tip of your tongue back slightly. The sides of your tongue should touch the inside of your top molar teeth. Make the sound without vibrating your vocal cords.

Words

INITIAL	MEDIAL	FINAL
she	di**rec**tion	wish
shore	**na**tion	**fi**nish
short	edu**ca**tion	fish
sheet	es**pe**cially	fresh
sure	**spe**cial	**Bri**tish

Sentences

1. I wish these sheets weren't so short.
2. You can buy fresh fish near the shore.
3. I'm not sure where I should get my education.
4. Can you give me directions to the British National Bank?
5. She won a special prize for finishing first.

/š/ shape

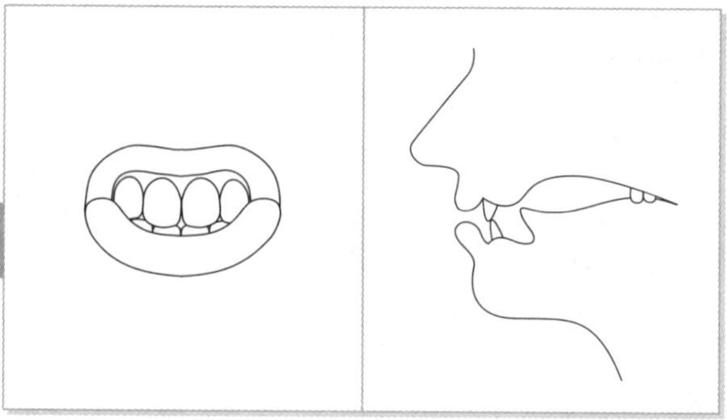

Day 2

To make the /š/ sound, form the shape of the /s/ sound with your mouth. Then round your lips and pull the tip of your tongue back slightly. The sides of your tongue should touch the inside of your top molar teeth. Make the sound without vibrating your vocal cords.

Words

INITIAL	MEDIAL	FINAL
shape	infor**ma**tion	brush
shown	ma**chine**	wash
shall	**o**cean	es**ta**blish
shoulder	**ac**tion	bush
sharp	a**ddi**tion	dish

Sentences

1. She brushed her hair over her shoulder.
2. The ocean shapes the shoreline.
3. I need information about washing machines.
4. The government established a new social action policy.
5. He showed me the sharp thorns on the bushes.

/s/ & /š/ sell-shell

Review

Practice distinguishing between the /s/ and /š/ sounds. Remember that the /s/ sound is formed with the tip of your tongue near the ridge that is behind your upper front teeth while the /š/ sound is formed with rounded lips and your tongue pulled back a little further and touching your mouth on the sides.

Words

INITIAL	MEDIAL	FINAL
sell - shell	last - lashed	lease - leash
sip - ship	**fa**stened - **fa**shioned	mass - mash
cells - shells	crust - crushed	a**ccom**plice - a**ccom**plish
sake - shake	fist - fished	gas - gash
so - show	**par**cel - **par**tial	Swiss - swish

Sentences

1. What sort of ship will you sail on?
2. Don't shake the parcel, or you'll crush the fragile glasses.
3. Could you show me where the gas station is?
4. I've only seen one TV show in the last several months.
5. What should I accomplish this semester?

/č/ change

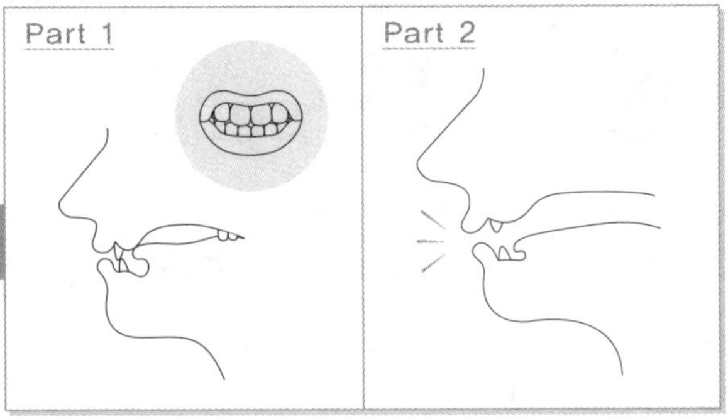

To make the /č/ sound, press the entire front of your tongue against the top of your mouth along the ridge that is behind your upper front teeth. The sides of your tongue should touch the inside of your top molar teeth. Round your lips. Release your tongue and let it drop without vibrating your vocal cords. Let the air escape against the back of your upper teeth.

Words

INITIAL	MEDIAL	FINAL
change	**pic**ture	each
children	**ques**tion	such
check	**na**tural	which
child	**tea**cher	catch
choose	**tem**perature	watch

Sentences

1. The teacher asked each child a question.
2. Choose which picture you like best.
3. Children have such natural curiosity.
4. When the temperature changes, it's easy to catch a cold.
5. She wrote a check when she purchased her new watch.

/ǰ/ join

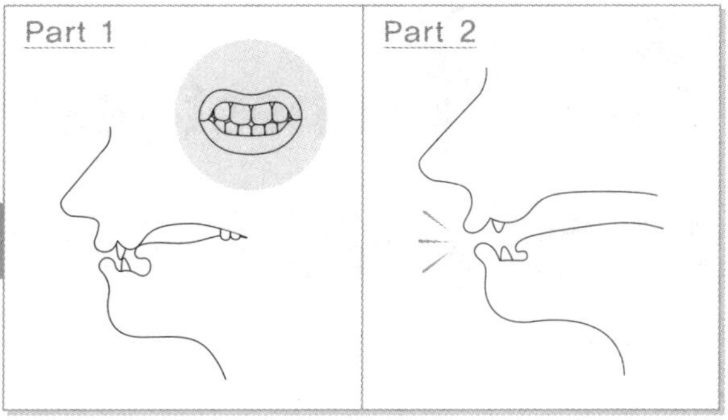

To make the /ǰ/ sound, form the shape of the /č/ sound with your mouth. Make the same sound, this time vibrating your vocal cords.

Words

INITIAL	MEDIAL	FINAL
join	**ob**ject	**lang**uage
jack	**en**gine	page
John	**e**nergy	age
German	**lar**ger	edge
general	**re**gion	strange

Sentences

1. The German general controlled a large region in Europe.
2. What is that strange object on the edge of the desk?
3. John has enough energy to study two languages.
4. Children of all ages can join the juggling class.
5. Lift the jeep up with a jack so I can see under the engine.

/č/ & /ǰ/ chest-jest

Review

Practice distinguishing between the /č/ and /ǰ/ sounds. Remember that the formation of the mouth is the same for these two sounds. /č/ is the sound formed without vibrating your vocal cords. /ǰ/ is the sound formed while vibrating your vocal cords.

Words

INITIAL	MEDIAL	FINAL
chest - jest	**sear**ching - **sur**ging	lunch - lunge
cheer - jeer	**e**tching - **e**dging	cinch - singe
choice - Joyce	**ri**ches - **ri**dges	perch - purge
chain - Jane	**per**ching - **pur**ging	be**seech** - be**seige**
chew - Jew	**ba**tches - **ba**dges	March - Marge

Sentences

1. Joyce, please put the dog back on its chain.
2. I said it in jest, but the child didn't think my joke was funny.
3. Hey, Jane! What's for lunch?
4. I've been searching for a new car for ages now.
5. I became a Jew by choice.

-/č/ endings

Make the /č/ sound at the end of each word. Once your tongue is released, quickly stop the air from flowing through your open mouth.

Words

FINAL /č/

inch	search	**re**search
rich	pitch	stretch
speech	teach	porch
reach	ranch	coach
branch	French	switch

Sentences

1. The preacher gave a speech in French.
2. "I will teach you how to pitch," the coach said.
3. The researcher found the ranch rich in oil.
4. I want to stretch out on the porch and take a nap.
5. The inchworm searched for food on the branch.

-/ǰ/ endings

Make the /ǰ/ sound at the end of each word. Once your tongue is released, quickly stop the air from flowing through your open mouth.

Words

FINAL /ǰ/

range	stage	**cour**age
huge	bridge	**or**ange
knowledge	charge	a**rrange**
average	cage	judge
George	**co**llege	**pa**ssage

Sentences

1. George charged across the bridge.
2. Can you arrange to find a large cage for my parrot?
3. A judge needs knowledge to grant justice.
4. In college, my grades were just average.
5. She read a passage from *The Red Badge of Courage.*

/Z/ zebra

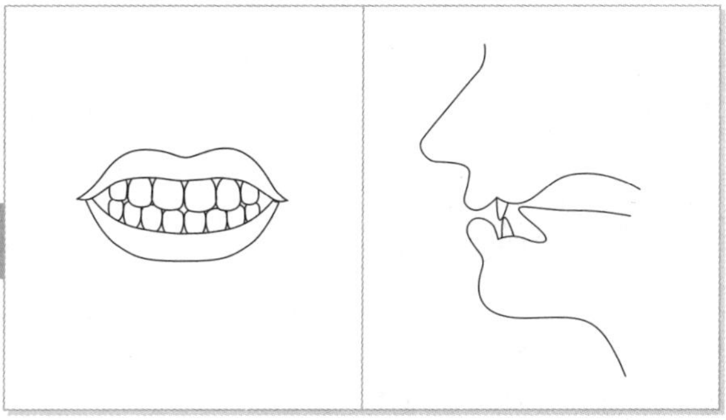

● Review

Review the /z/ sound. Remember that the /z/ sound is made by biting your teeth together gently and raising the tip of your tongue toward the top of your mouth along the ridge that is behind your upper front teeth without touching it.

Words

INITIAL	MEDIAL	FINAL
zebra	**bus**iness	those
zoom	**ea**sily	use
zap	**i**sn't	was
Zionist	**wa**sn't	goes
Zim**ba**bwe	**doe**sn't	size

Sentences

1. He goes to Zimbabwe to see zebras every year.
2. He doesn't want to use our business proposal.
3. The zap wasn't powerful, but it was painful.
4. I can easily find those shoes in a larger size.
5. I was able to zip right through the PowerPoint presentation.

/ǰ/ jar

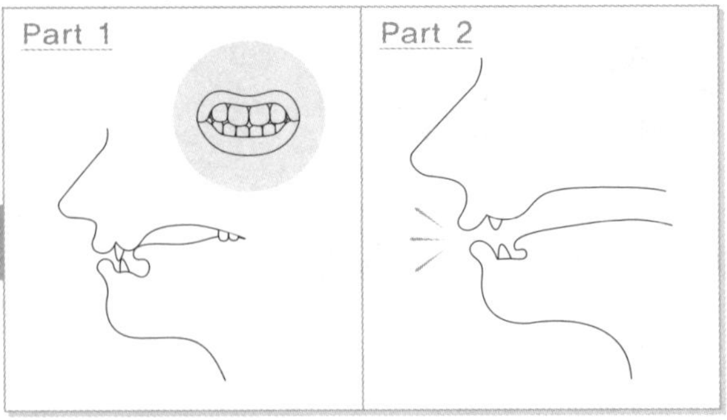

● Review

Review the /ǰ/ sound. Remember that the /ǰ/ sound is made by pressing the entire front of your tongue against the top of your mouth along the ridge that is behind your upper front teeth. The sides of your tongue should touch the inside of your top molar teeth. Round your lips. Vibrate your vocal cords, release your tongue, and let it drop. Let the air escape against the back of your upper teeth.

Words	INITIAL	MEDIAL	FINAL
	jar	en**joy**	**pa**ckage
	Jim	**lar**gest	**voy**age
	giant	**ima**gine	**da**mage
	generally	**ma**jor	ex**change**
	Germany	o**rig**inal	**i**mage

Sentences

1. I bought a large jar of strawberry jam.
2. The image was more beautiful than I had originally imagined.
3. I enjoy watching Major League Baseball™, especially the Giants.
4. The package was damaged on its voyage.
5. We generally host exchange students from Germany.

/z/ & /ǰ/ zest-jest

● Review

Practice distinguishing between the /z/ and /ǰ/ sounds. Remember that the /z/ sound is formed with only the tip of your tongue near the ridge that is behind your upper front teeth while the /ǰ/ sound is formed with rounded lips and the entire front of your tongue against the ridge that is behind your upper front teeth.

Words

INITIAL	MEDIAL	FINAL
zest - jest	gazed - gauged	chains - change
zealous - **jea**lous	**rea**son - **re**gion	**do**ses - **do**sage
zone - Joan	**bu**zzing - **bu**dging	**me**sses - **me**ssage
zoos - Jews	**rai**sing - **ra**ging	twins - twinge
Z - G	**sei**zes - **sie**ges	pays - page

Sentences

1. Raising twins means changing a lot of diapers.
2. I felt a twinge of jealousy when I saw Joan's new jacket.
3. If the conversation becomes unpleasant, just change the topic.
4. She pays twice as much in taxes because of the region she lives in.
5. He doesn't have any reason to ignore my message.

/ž/ genre

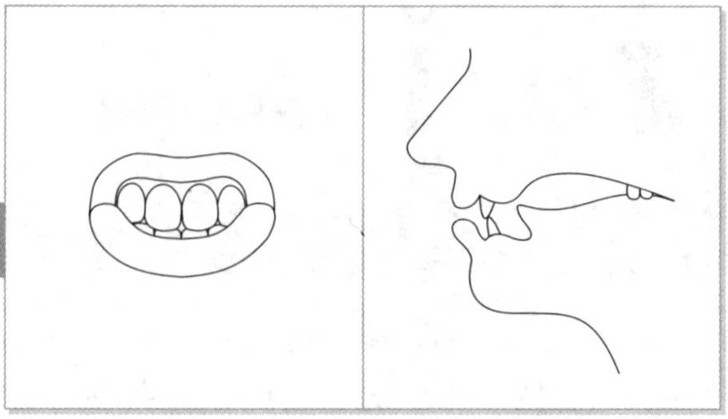

● Day 1

To make the /ž/ sound, form the shape of the /š/ sound with your mouth. Make the same sound, this time vibrating your vocal cords.

Words

INITIAL	MEDIAL	FINAL
genre	**u**sually	ma**ssage**
	measure	mi**rage**
	television	pre**stige**
	usual	rouge
	Asia	beige

Sentences

1. I dozed off while watching my usual television program.
2. How do you measure prestige in Asia?
3. I massaged my eyes to get rid of the mirage.
4. She used a beige-colored rouge to color her cheeks.
5. What genre of movies do you usually watch?

/ž/ genre

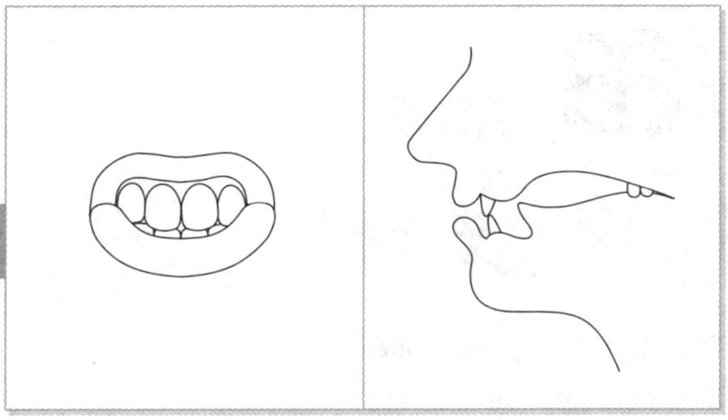

● Day 2

To make the /ž/ sound, form the shape of the /š/ sound with your mouth. Make the same sound, this time vibrating your vocal cords.

Words	INITIAL	MEDIAL	FINAL
	genre	di**vi**sion	co**llage**
		un**u**sual	cor**sage**
		o**ccas**ionally	entour**age**
		de**ci**sions	mon**tage**
		measurements	luge

Sentences

1. I occasionally have to make decisions when there is division.
2. A luge is an unusual racing sled.
3. We used long division to find the exact measurements.
4. A montage is a movie collage.
5. They bought a corsage for every woman in the entourage.

/æ/ ask

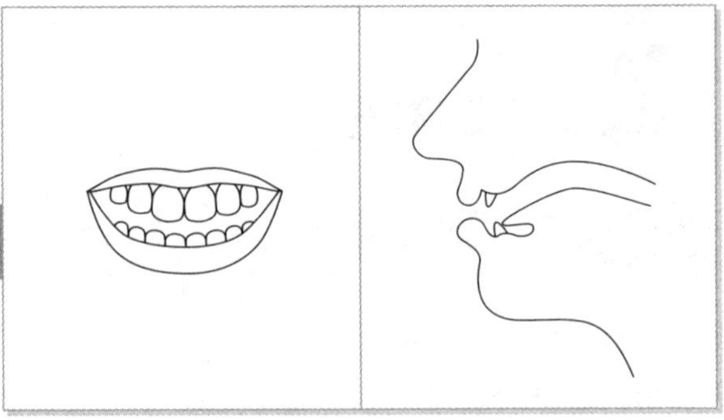

●Day 1

To make the /æ/ sound, open your mouth and spread your lips. Let the tip of your tongue rest against the back of your lower teeth. When you make this sound, your face and jaw should be relaxed.

Words	INITIAL	MEDIAL	FINAL
	ask	had	*none*
	action	man	
	animal	hand	
	after**noon**	be**gan**	
	Africa	can't	

Sentences

1. I can't imagine how many animals live in Africa.
2. The man asked for her hand in marriage.
3. I had an awful afternoon.
4. We need to establish a new plan of action.
5. I began to realize that my dad really had loved me.

/æ/ apple

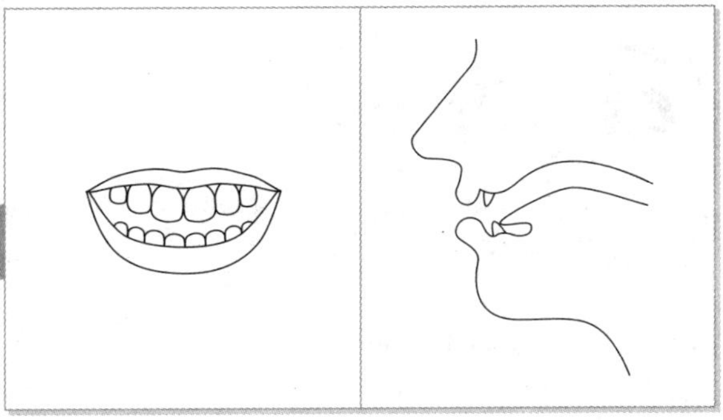

Day 2

To make the /æ/ sound, open your mouth and spread your lips. Let the tip of your tongue rest against the back of your lower teeth. When you make this sound, your face and jaw should be relaxed.

Words

INITIAL	MEDIAL	FINAL
apple	fact	*none*
added	map	
ac**ti**vities	**ma**tter	
atmosphere	**pa**ttern	
actually	plant	

Sentences

1. As a matter of fact, I feel sad.
2. The apple seed grew into a scraggly little plant.
3. Actually, the atmosphere at my workplace is positive.
4. They've added more activities to the afternoon schedule.
5. There's a pattern to this treasure map.

/a/ officer

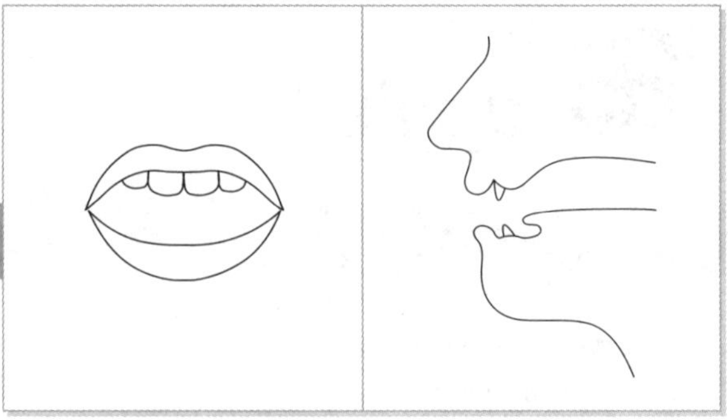

To make the /a/ sound, open your mouth wide and drop your jaw. Rest your tongue on the bottom of your mouth without touching your teeth. When you make this sound, your face and jaw should be relaxed.

Words

INITIAL	MEDIAL	FINAL
officer	not	*none*
ope**ra**tion	got	
oxygen	**bo**dy	
oppor**tu**nity	ca**nnot**	
Oc**to**ber	**bo**ttom	

Sentences

1. I got the opportunity to sing in an octet.
2. She did not have the operation in October.
3. The officer was ordered to search the bottom of the pond.
4. I've got a lot to do before I get off work.
5. The human body cannot live without oxygen.

/æ/ & /a/ add-odd

Review

Practice distinguishing between the /æ/ and /a/ sounds. Remember that the /æ/ sound is formed with your lips spread and your tongue touching your bottom teeth while the /a/ sound is formed with your jaw dropped and your tongue not touching your bottom teeth.

Words	INITIAL	MEDIAL	FINAL
	add - odd	bag - bog	*none*
	active - **oc**tave	band - bond	
	apt - opt	**ba**ttle - **bo**ttle	
	ax - ox	cat - cot	
		packet - **po**cket	

Sentences

1. Last night I saw my favorite rock band in concert.
2. Ann has a strong bond with her dad.
3. Admitting that you have a problem is half the battle.
4. Please hand me a packet of sugar for my coffee.
5. She often keeps a bottle of aspirin in her bag.

/ar/ arm

To make the /ar/ sound, form the shape of the /a/ sound with your mouth. Vibrate your vocal cords and immediately press the sides of your tongue against the inside of your back molar teeth, forming the /r/ sound.

Words	INITIAL	MEDIAL	FINAL
	arm	hard	far
	art	dark	**ra**dar
	aren't	heart	car
	army	start	bar
	article	farm	star

Sentences

1. You've worked hard to get this far in the field of art.
2. The dark bruises on her arms aren't from an accident.
3. Police armed with radar guns caught the speeding cars.
4. I read a heart-rending article about farmers in the newspaper.
5. A five-star general led the army at the start of the war.

/ɛ/ enter

Day 1

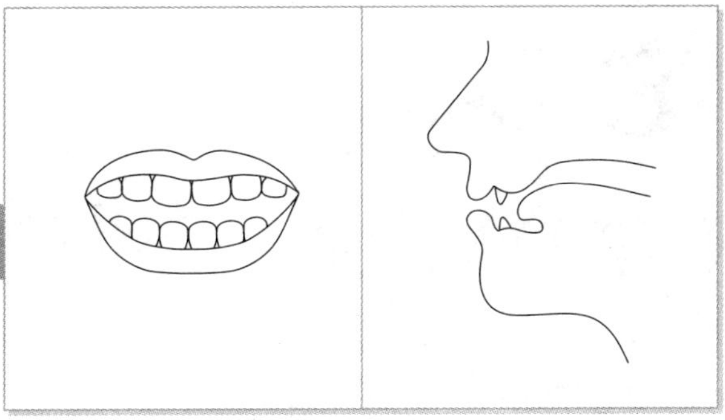

To make the /ɛ/ sound, open your mouth and spread your lips a little. Place your tongue, with the sides slightly curled upward, near the front of your mouth. When you make this sound, your face and jaw should be relaxed.

Words	INITIAL	MEDIAL	FINAL
	enter	men	*none*
	enemy	next	
	exercise	**ma**ny	
	edu**ca**tion	said	
	any	a**gain**	

Sentences

1. "I paid next to nothing for my education," Emily said.
2. There are many different exercises for strengthening your arms.
3. Our men met the enemy soldiers outside the village.
4. Let's try to finish by the end of next week.
5. Will I have any chance to see you again before you head to California?

/ɛ/ empty

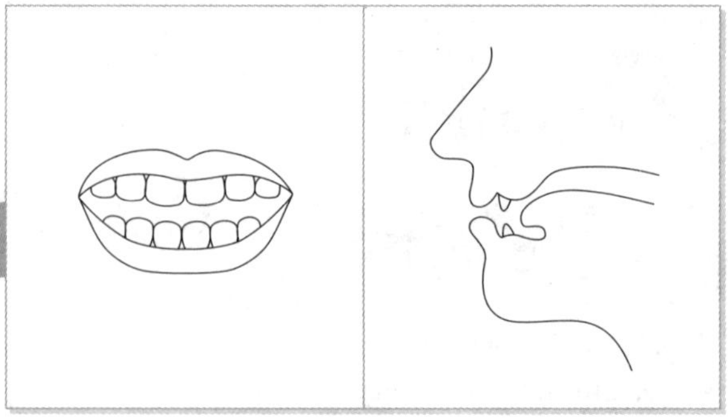

● Day 2

To make the /ɛ/ sound, open your mouth and spread your lips a little. Place your tongue, with the sides slightly curled upward, near the front of your mouth. When you make this sound, your face and jaw should be relaxed.

Words

INITIAL	MEDIAL	FINAL
empty	went	*none*
element	when	
extra	how**e**ver	
everywhere	let	
anyone	**se**cond	

Sentences

1. My mind went blank when the teacher asked me a question.
2. Let's take a little extra time to get to know him.
3. She was never mean to anyone but herself.
4. The imperceptible elements of our universe are everywhere.
5. The second step is difficult. However, it is not impossible.

/æ/ activity

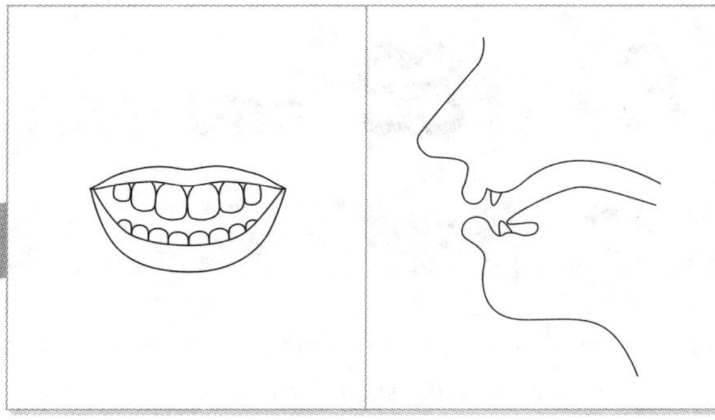

Review

Review the /æ/ sound. Remember that the /æ/ sound is made by opening your mouth and spreading your lips. Lightly press the tip of your tongue against the back of your lower teeth. When you make this sound, your face and jaw should be relaxed.

Words

INITIAL	MEDIAL	FINAL
ac**ti**vity	sat	*none*
accident	stand	
adjective	that's	
alphabet	ex**ac**tly	
Andy	flat	

Sentences

1. I can't stand eating in the cafeteria.
2. That's exactly how it happened.
3. Andy was badly injured in a tragic accident.
4. In this activity, we will practice writing the alphabet.
5. *Even* is an adjective that can mean *flat* or *smooth.*

/ɛ/ & /æ/ end-and

Review

Practice distinguishing between the /ɛ/ and /æ/ sounds. Remember that the /ɛ/ sound is formed with your tongue, slightly curled, near the front of your mouth while the /æ/ sound is formed with your tongue lightly pressed against the back of your lower teeth.

Words

INITIAL	MEDIAL	FINAL
end - and	bed - bad	*none*
excess - **ac**cess	kept - capped	
ember - **am**ber	**ke**ttle - **ca**ttle	
N - Ann	dead - dad	
Ellen - **A**llen	leg - lag	

Sentences

1. Ellen had a bad day.
2. Allen went into the kitchen and put the kettle on.
3. A woman at the back kept making rude comments.
4. Ann has access to many exciting events.
5. My cat likes to sleep at the head of my bed.

/ɛr/ airplane

To make the /ɛr/ sound, form the shape of the /ɛ/ sound with your mouth. Vibrate your vocal cords and immediately press the sides of your tongue against the inside of your back molar teeth, forming the /r/ sound.

Words	INITIAL	MEDIAL	FINAL
	airplane	**carr**y	where
	area	**ne**cessary	care
	airport	there's	square
	errors	**Mar**y	com**pare**
	era	A**meri**ca	share

Sentences

1. Are there any stores in this area that carry English magazines?
2. There's no need to stress out about a few errors, Sharon.
3. Please take care of Mary while she's in South America.
4. I can share my software with you, if necessary.
5. Compare the prices of each airline flying into that airport.

/I/ in

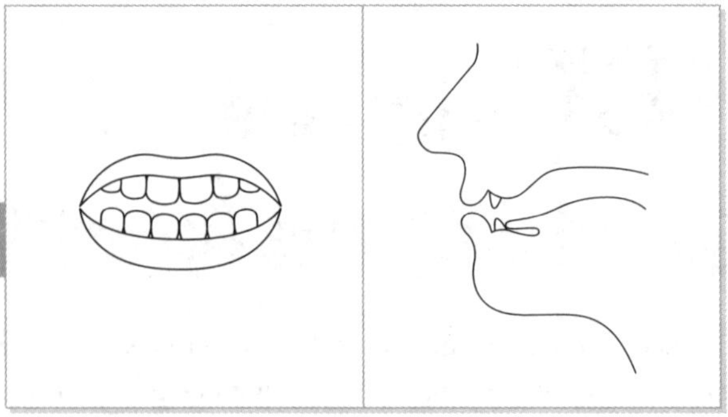

Day 1

To make the /I/ sound, open your mouth a little and pull your lips back into a tight smile. Raise the sides of your tongue toward the top of your mouth inside your upper teeth as high as you can without touching it. Allow the tip of your tongue to touch the back of your lower teeth. Then, keeping the same position with your tongue, relax your face and jaw. Vibrate your vocal cords.

Words

INITIAL	MEDIAL	FINAL
in	him	*none*
interest	**di**dn't	
in**clude**	un**til**	
issue	wind	
inter**na**tional	Bill	

Sentences

1. Are you interested in him?
2. Don't tell Bill until the last minute.
3. Why didn't you include any pictures in your letter?
4. I invited your cousin Lynn to the international fair.
5. Why is wind power such an important issue?

/I/ indeed

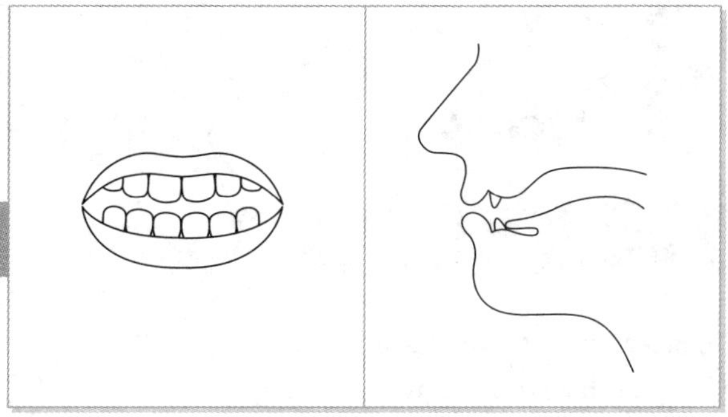

● Day 2

To make the /I/ sound, open your mouth a little and pull your lips back into a tight smile. Raise the sides of your tongue toward the top of your mouth inside your upper teeth as high as you can without touching it. Allow the tip of your tongue to touch the back of your lower teeth. Then, keeping the same position with your tongue, relax your face and jaw. Vibrate your vocal cords.

Words	INITIAL	MEDIAL	FINAL
	in**deed**	build	*none*
	instrument	po**li**tical	
	income	**quick**ly	
	in**creased**	**sys**tem	
	in**dus**trial	**wo**men	

Sentences

1. He has a six-figure income.
2. It's difficult to build musical instruments by hand.
3. Our political system is based on the supreme right of the people.
4. The Industrial Revolution increased our ability to produce goods quickly.
5. Relationships between women and men are different in different cultures.

/i/ east

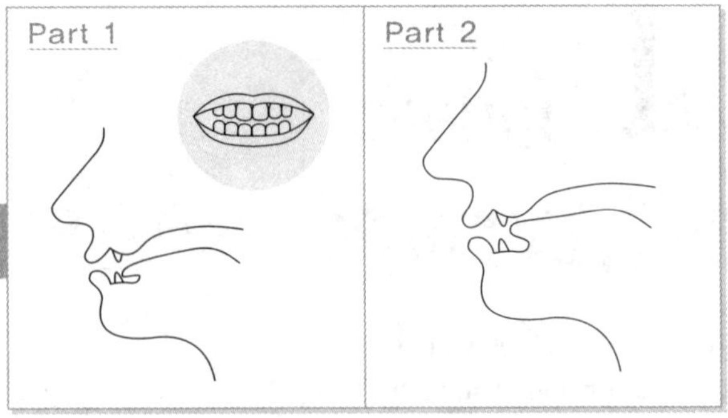

To make the /i/ sound, open your mouth a little and pull your lips back into a tight smile. Raise the sides of your tongue toward the top of your mouth inside your upper teeth as high as you can without touching it. Allow the tip of your tongue to touch the back of your lower teeth. Begin vibrating your vocal cords and pull the front of your tongue closer to the top of your mouth. When you make this sound, your face, jaw and throat should be tense.

Words

INITIAL	MEDIAL	FINAL
east	be**tween**	me
equal	feel	he
easier	**be**ing	we
evening	feet	**mo**ney
eager	i**de**a	**stor**y

Sentences

1. Let me see how much money I have.
2. It would be much easier if we took a taxi.
3. He stepped in between my father and me.
4. It feels like we're not being treated equally.
5. We took a walk down East Avenue last evening.

/I/ & /i/ it-eat

● Review

Practice distinguishing between the /I/ and /i/ sounds. Remember that the formation of the mouth is similar for these two sounds. /I/ is the sound formed with a relaxed face and jaw. /i/ is the sound formed with a tense face and jaw and the tongue pulled a little closer to the top of the mouth.

Words	INITIAL	MEDIAL	FINAL
	it - eat	bin - bean	*none*
	itch - each	lick - leak	
	is - ease	knit - neat	
	it's - eats	hid - he'd	
		pitch - peach	

Sentences

1. I'll deal with it.
2. We filled our bowls with ice cream.
3. The class is taking a field trip today.
4. He'd better finish his homework.
5. Almost a million people become ill each year from parasites.

/Ir/ ears

To make the /Ir/ sound, form the shape of the /I/ sound with your mouth. Vibrate your vocal cords and immediately press the sides of your tongue against your back molar teeth, forming the /r/ sound.

Words

INITIAL	MEDIAL	FINAL
ears	**near**ly	dear
ear	ma**ter**ial	we're
irre**spec**tive	**per**iod	year
irri**ta**tion	**clear**ly	near
irre**sis**tible	near**by**	clear

Sentences

1. I have worn hearing aids for nearly ten years.
2. Kira, dear, we're worried about you.
3. She smiles ear-to-ear whenever her husband is near.
4. The noise from the nearby construction irritated my aching ears.
5. She's always irresistibly cheerful, irrespective of the circumstances.

LEVEL 3

/f/ & /θ/ free-three

Review

Practice distinguishing between the /f/ and /θ/ sounds. Remember that the /f/ sound is formed using your upper teeth and lower lip while the /θ/ sound is formed with the tip of your tongue between your teeth.

Words

INITIAL	MEDIAL	FINAL
free - three	**deaf**ly - **death**ly	miff - myth
first - thirst	re**fresh** - re**thresh**	deaf - death
fought - thought	**roo**fless - **ruth**less	oaf - oath
fin - thin	re**fought** - re**thought**	reef - wreath
frill - thrill		roof - Ruth

Sentences

1. He became deaf at the age of three after falling from a roof.
2. When I first saw her, she was deathly thin.
3. I have always thought that Joseph Stalin was a ruthless man.
4. The man fought to the death for his beliefs.
5. Ruth was thrilled at the chance to scuba dive near the reef.

/s/ & /š/ save-shave

Review

Practice distinguishing between the /s/ and /š/ sounds. Remember that the /s/ sound is formed with the tip of your tongue near the ridge that is behind your upper front teeth while the /š/ sound is formed with rounded lips and your tongue pulled back a little further and touching your mouth on the sides.

Words

INITIAL	MEDIAL	FINAL
save - shave	fist - fished	mess - mesh
sell - shell	**ma**sses - **ma**shes	plus - plush
sign - shine	**par**cel - **par**tial	class - clash
single - **shin**gle	**fa**sten - **fa**shion	**i**ris - **I**rish
seed - she'd	**ha**sten - **Hai**tian	lease - leash

Sentences

1. Shave your head. You'll save time by not having to wash your hair.
2. She'd kill me if I told a single person.
3. I fished through the trash until I found the missing paper.
4. I'm partial to science-fiction novels.
5. That store sells the latest fashions from Paris.

/č/ & /t/ chalk-talk

Review

Practice distinguishing between the /č/ and /t/ sounds. Remember that the /č/ sound is formed with rounded lips and the entire front of your tongue along the ridge that is behind your upper front teeth while the /t/ sound is formed with open lips and only the tip of your tongue along the ridge that is behind your upper front teeth.

Words

INITIAL	MEDIAL	FINAL
chalk - talk	**tea**cher - **tee**ter	hatch - hat
chart - tart	**coa**ching - **coa**ting	hitch - hit
chased - taste	**mar**cher - **mar**tyr	hunch - hunt
cheers - tears	**ges**ture - **jes**ter	ouch - out
chose - toes	**pas**ture - **pas**tor	starch - start

Sentences

1. I'm going to talk to my teacher after class.
2. She chased after the boy who stole her hat.
3. The catchy new song hit the charts at number one.
4. The man's rude gesture brought the woman to tears.
5. I need to buy more chalk, but I'm out of money.

/z/ & /ǰ/ zest-jest

● Review

Practice distinguishing between the /z/ and /ǰ/ sounds. Remember that the /z/ sound is formed with only the tip of your tongue near the ridge that is behind your upper front teeth while the /ǰ/ sound is formed with rounded lips and the entire front of your tongue against the ridge that is behind your upper front teeth.

Words

INITIAL	MEDIAL	FINAL
zest - jest	**rea**sons - **re**gions	stays - stage
zealous - **jea**lous	**fra**zzle - **fra**gile	**u**ses - **u**sage
zone - Joan	gazed - gauged	twins - twinge
zoo - Jew	**rai**sing - **ra**ging	rains - range
Zeus - juice	**fu**zzy - **fu**dgy	**me**sses - **me**ssage

Sentences

1. "What happens here, stays here," said Joan.
2. She is tired of her husband's jealous rages.
3. Zane adds a lot of zest to his stage productions.
4. The war in Vietnam was still raging when I was young.
5. All eyes gazed upon the fragile boy's face.

/d/ & /ð/ day-they

● Review

Practice distinguishing between the /d/ and /ð/ sounds. Remember that the /d/ sound is formed with the tip of your tongue touching the ridge that is behind your upper front teeth while the /ð/ sound is formed with the tip of your tongue between your teeth.

Words

INITIAL	MEDIAL	FINAL
day - they	**bree**ding - **brea**thing	laid - lathe
die - thy	**ri**ding - **wri**thing	tide - tithe
dare - their	**u**dder - **o**ther	reed - wreathe
den - then	**la**dder - **la**ther	sued - soothe
dough - though	**wor**dy - **wor**thy	side - scythe

Sentences

1. Though the weather was cold, the jockey still went riding.
2. The women were condemned to die for their crime.
3. Watching the tide rise and fall soothes my worried mind.
4. They sued me for slander.
5. I wanted to be worthy of her hand.

/d/ & /r/ detail-retail

Review

Practice distinguishing between the /d/ and /r/ sounds. Remember that the /d/ sound is formed by touching the ridge that is behind your upper front teeth with the tip of your tongue while the /r/ sound is formed by pressing the sides of your tongue against the inside of your upper back molar teeth.

Words

INITIAL	MEDIAL	FINAL
detail - **re**tail	odes - oars	road - roar
de**fer** - re**fer**	over**done** - over**run**	toad - tore
de**port** - re**port**	unde**ceived** - unre**ceived**	died - dire
de**sign** - re**sign**	undi**ssolved** - unre**solved**	cod - car
decent - **re**cent	un**da**ted - un**ra**ted	code - core

Sentences

1. The post office said that my letter was unreceived.
2. Koreans don't usually refer to each other by their given name.
3. I was sad to hear that your grandma died yesterday.
4. My car broke down last week.
5. Ryan described the recent developments in great detail.

/r/ & /l/ rice-lice

● Review

Practice distinguishing between the /r/ and /l/ sounds. Remember that the /r/ sound is formed using the sides of your tongue while the /l/ sound is formed using the tip of your tongue.

Words

INITIAL	MEDIAL	FINAL
rice - lice	brush - blush	roar - roll
rather - **la**ther	fries - flies	gore - goal
wrapped - lapped	frog - flog	store - stole
rise - lies	grew - glue	four - foal
writer - **ligh**ter	**pi**rate - **pi**lot	more - mole

Sentences

1. The chocolate heart was wrapped in plastic.
2. Brush your long hair thoroughly before you wash it.
3. A bowl of rice has less fat than an order of french fries.
4. Let's play a game of leap frog.
5. I'd rather be a pilot than a pirate.

/æ/ & /I/ as-is

● Review

Practice distinguishing between the /æ/ and /I/ sounds. Remember that the /æ/ sound is formed with your mouth open and your lips spread while the /I/ sound is formed with your mouth only slightly open and the sides of your tongue curved upward.

Words

INITIAL	MEDIAL	FINAL
as - is	dash - dish	*none*
an**ter**ior - in**ter**ior	lack - lick	
at - it	slap - slip	
Al - ill	**ba**bysat - **ba**bysit	
Ann - in	unin**ha**bited - unin**hi**bited	

Sentences

1. Let's have someone babysit the kids tonight.
2. Ann happened to order the most expensive dish on the menu.
3. The island is uninhabited and difficult to access.
4. Al works for the Ministry of the Interior.
5. I slipped into class at the last minute.

/i/ & /ɛ/ each-etch

Review

Practice distinguishing between the /i/ and /ɛ/ sounds. Remember that the /i/ sound is formed with a tense face and jaw and the front of your tongue pulled close to the top of your mouth while the /ɛ/ sound is formed with your mouth open, your lips slightly spread, and your tongue, slightly curled, near the front of your mouth.

Words

INITIAL	MEDIAL	FINAL
each - etch	feed - fed	*none*
eel - L	geese - guess	
Easter - **Es**ther	meet - met	
	reader - **re**dder	
	weed - wed	

Sentences

1. We sell brown eggs from chickens fed with organic feed.
2. You'll never guess who I met last week.
3. Seal the envelope and leave it on the table for Esther.
4. It's been ten years since we've seen each other.
5. I'm meeting my son Greg for Easter brunch.

/a/ & /I/ on-in

Review

Practice distinguishing between the /a/ and /I/ sounds. Remember that the /a/ sound is formed with your jaw dropped and your tongue not touching your bottom teeth while the /I/ sound is formed with your mouth only slightly open and the sides of your tongue curved upward.

Words	INITIAL	MEDIAL	FINAL
	on - in	**ro**tten - **wri**tten	*none*
	onset - **in**set	drop - drip	
	onto - **in**to	wash - wish	
	onward - **in**ward	**co**tton - **ki**tten	
	honor - **i**nner	not - knit	

Sentences

1. I wish I had not done it.
2. He held the kitten on his lap.
3. You should wash that cotton knit sweater in cold water.
4. It is a great honor to be in the president's inner circle.
5. Toss the rotten lettuce into the garbage.

/g/ game

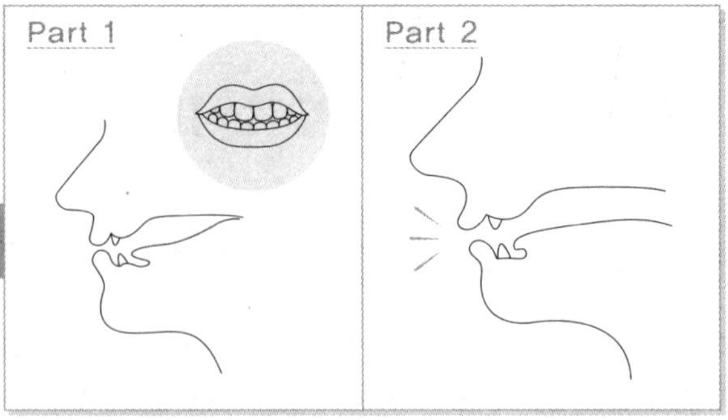

To make the /g/ sound, press the back of your tongue firmly against the top of your mouth in the very back. While vibrating your vocal cords, release your tongue and drop your jaw with a puff of air.

Words

INITIAL	MEDIAL	FINAL
game	a**go**	flag
go	be**gi**nning	dug
girl	**su**gar	log
ground	**re**gular	fog
getting	**fi**gure	dig

Sentences

1. The Olympic Games had their beginning in Greece.
2. A few months ago, the girl wrote a poem about her country's flag.
3. I need to go to the store to get more sugar.
4. The Garcia family dug a foundation for their new log cabin.
5. The fog is getting so thick that we can't see where we're going.

/k/ can

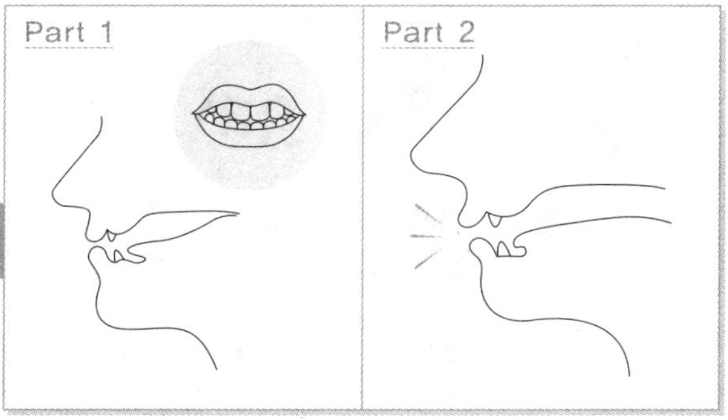

To make the /k/ sound, form the shape of the /g/ sound with your mouth. Make the same sound, this time without vibrating your vocal cords.

Words	INITIAL	MEDIAL	FINAL
	can	be**came**	make
	came	**ma**king	book
	come	school	took
	cut	sky	walk
	kind	**ta**ken	mark

Sentences

1. I wish I could make all your dreams come true.
2. The girl took her cat to school for show-and-tell.
3. Can you carry all of those books okay?
4. The sky had a kind of pinkish tint to it.
5. Would you like to come on a walk with me?

/g/ & /k/ gave-cave

● Review

Practice distinguishing between the /g/ and /k/ sounds. Remember that the formation of the mouth is the same for these two sounds. /g/ is the sound formed while vibrating your vocal cords. /k/ is the sound formed without vibrating your vocal cords.

Words

INITIAL	MEDIAL	FINAL
gave - cave	de**gree** - de**cree**	lug - luck
glows - close	**lo**gging - **lo**cking	dog - dock
grow - crow	**bi**gger - **bi**cker	pig - pick
goal - coal	pre**glued** - pre**clude**	tag - tack
ghost - coast	**de**legate - **de**licate	snag - snack

Sentences

1. His work gave him a great sense of accomplishment.
2. You need a good degree of luck to see a bear in Korea.
3. The logging road passes close to the mouth of a large cave.
4. Your pig keeps getting bigger and bigger.
5. My dog has a delicate stomach.

/ks/ exciting

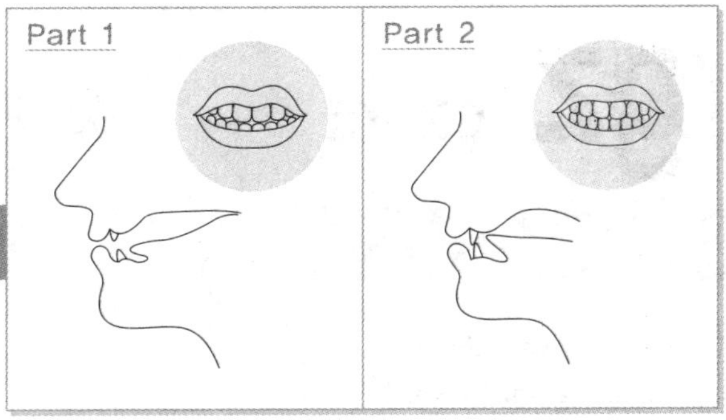

The letter *x* is sometimes pronounced as /ks/. To make the /ks/ sound, form the /k/ sound with your mouth. Release your jaw with a puff of air. Then immediately raise the tip of your tongue toward the the ridge that is behind your upper front teeth, forming the /s/ sound. No vowel sound is added before the /s/.

Words

INITIAL	MEDIAL	FINAL
none	ex**ci**ting	box
	ex**pre**ssion	mix
	ex**cite**ment	tax
	Mexico	fix
	Texas	**com**plex

Sentences

1. Your trip to Mexico must have been very exciting.
2. Get me a box of muffin mix while you're out.
3. His face had an expression of confusion rather than excitement.
4. The government needs to fix the unfair tax system.
5. I live in an apartment complex in Austin, Texas.

/gz/ exact

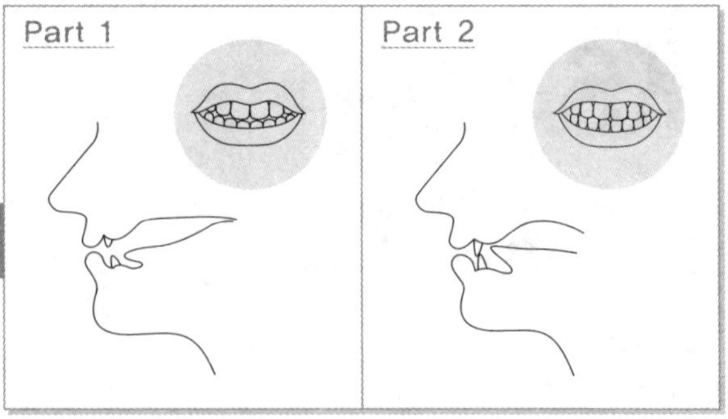

The letter *x* is sometimes pronounced as /gz/. To make the /gz/ sound, form the /g/ sound with your mouth. While vibrating your vocal cords, release your jaw with a puff of air. Then immediately raise the tip of your tongue toward the ridge that is behind your upper front teeth, forming the /z/ sound. No vowel sound is added before the /z/.

Words

INITIAL	MEDIAL	FINAL
none	ex**act**	eggs
	ex**a**mine	drugs
	ex**ist**	legs
	ex**am**ples	dogs
	Alex**an**der	bags

Sentences

1. The students had to examine fish eggs in biology class.
2. An extensive number of pain relief drugs now exists.
3. Dachshunds are dogs known for their short legs.
4. Tell me the exact time that Alexander woke up.
5. Let me give you some examples of the types of bags we sell.

/m/ my

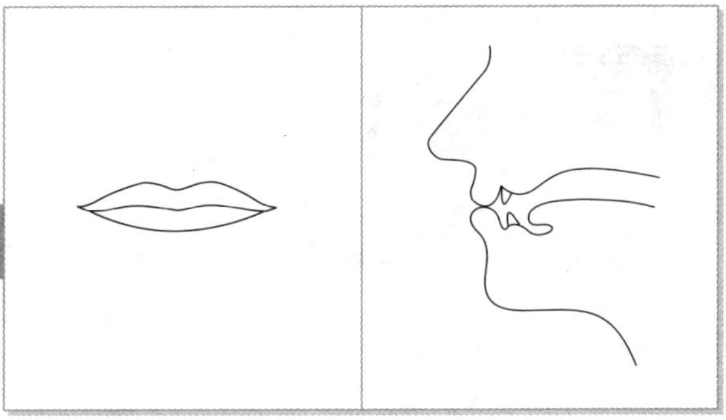

To make the /m/ sound, press your lips together. Vibrate your vocal cords and allow the sound to come out through your nose.

Words

INITIAL	MEDIAL	FINAL
my	**num**ber	home
may	a**mong**	name
might	**some**time	same
made	**co**ming	some
mean	**co**mmon	be**come**

Sentences

1. Give me your home phone number.
2. I might not change my name after I get married.
3. You've made the same mistake that you made yesterday.
4. I may need some help with my homework.
5. Depression is common among women after pregnancy.

/n/ night

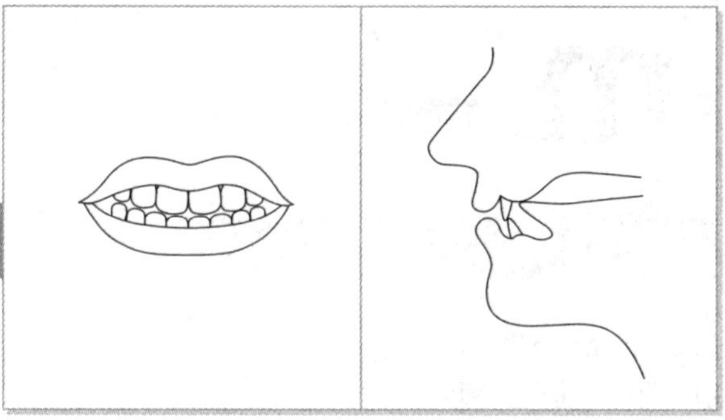

To make the /n/ sound, press the tip of your tongue against the top of your mouth along the ridge that is behind your upper front teeth. Vibrate your vocal cords and allow the sound to come out through your nose.

Words	INITIAL	MEDIAL	FINAL
	night	sound	an
	now	want	been
	know	front	one
	known	point	own
	New York	**fi**nally	**cer**tain

Sentences

1. Mind your own business.
2. Someday I want to work for an investment firm in New York City.
3. I've been meaning to tell you the news for a while now.
4. Tonight is my first time to perform in front of an audience.
5. I don't know what the point is.

/m/ & /n/ mice-nice

● Review

Practice distinguishing between the /m/ and /n/ sounds. Remember to allow both sounds to come out through your nose. The /m/ sound is formed with your lips pressed together while the /n/ sound is formed with the tip of your tongue against the top of your mouth along the ridge that is behind your upper front teeth.

Words

INITIAL	MEDIAL	FINAL
mice - nice	**di**mmer - **di**nner	firm - fern
messed - nest	**tu**mor - **tu**ner	mime - mine
mail - nail	**smu**ggle - **snu**ggle	scream - screen
motion - **no**tion	**foa**ming - **pho**ning	skim - skin
me - knee	**some**day - **Sun**day	term - turn

Sentences

1. Someday I'm going to stop biting my nails.
2. Would you have dinner with me on Sunday?
3. I'd like you to meet a friend of mine.
4. You can contact the law firm by email.
5. Michael scraped some skin off his knee when he fell.

/ŋ/ lungs

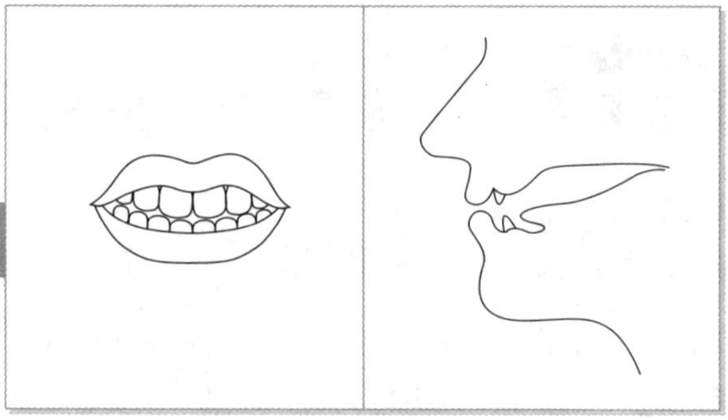

To make the /ŋ/ sound, form the shape of the /g/ sound with your mouth. Do not release your tongue. Instead, vibrate your vocal cords and allow the sound to come out through your nose.

Words	INITIAL	MEDIAL	FINAL
	none	lungs	**dur**ing
		things	**buil**ding
		in**crea**singly	**do**ing
		singing	**mo**ving
		Washington	strong

Sentences

1. I need to concentrate on stretching and building more muscle strength.
2. Smoking damages the lungs, making it increasingly difficult to breathe.
3. A strong storm is moving toward the coast, bringing with it heavy snowfall.
4. I'm planning to be in Washington during the week of May 12th-19th.
5. You should be doing something more productive than singing.

/ŋg/ anger
/ŋk/ monkey

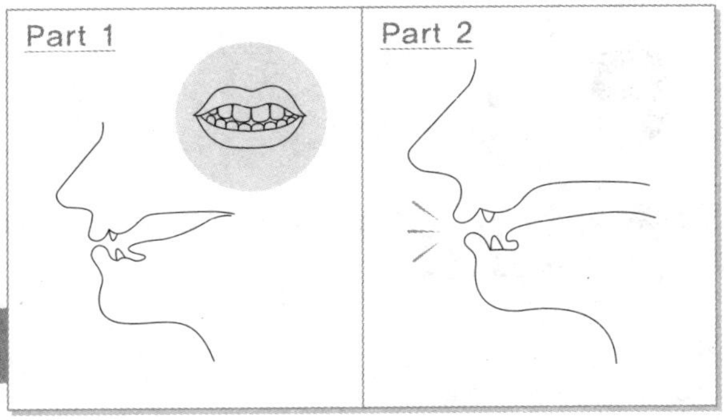

The sound /ŋ/ can be found in combination with the /g/ and /k/ sounds.

- To make the /ŋg/ sound, form the shape of the /ŋ/ sound with your mouth. Begin vibrating your vocal cords. Then release your tongue and drop your jaw with a puff of air, forming the /g/ sound.
- To make the /ŋk/ sound, form the shape of the /ŋ/ sound with your mouth. Begin vibrating your vocal cords. Then stop vibrating your vocal cords, release your tongue, and drop your jaw with a puff of air, forming the /k/ sound.

Words

/ŋg/ MEDIAL		/ŋk/ MEDIAL	/ŋk/ FINAL
anger	**tri**angle	**mon**key	pink
finger	**strong**er	**un**cle	thank
hungry	**young**er	**blan**ket	tank
congress	**jung**le	**func**tion	trunk
England	**long**er	**don**key	drunk

Sentences

1. Tell your uncle thank you for the pink sweater.
2. Monkeys use their nimble fingers to find food in the jungle.
3. I forgot my younger brother's blanket in the trunk of the car.
4. One function of Congress is to care for millions of hungry people.
5. England hopes to build a stronger defense by deploying more tanks.

/e/ ate

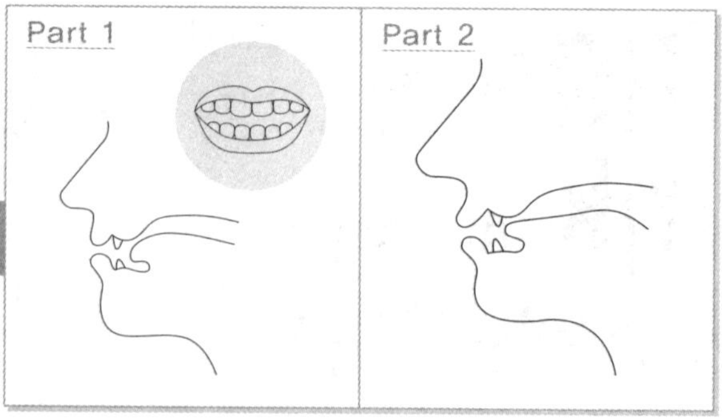

● Day 1

To make the /e/ sound, open your mouth and spread your lips a little. Place your tongue, with the sides slightly curled upward, near the front of your mouth. Begin vibrating your vocal cords and pull the front of your tongue closer to the top of your mouth, ending in an /i/ sound. When you make this sound, your face and jaw should be tense. Make the transition so quickly that you pronounce the sound as one syllable.

Words

INITIAL	MEDIAL	FINAL
ate	**ta**ble	a**way**
able	main	say
ancient	state	way
aid	**ba**by	to**day**
April	case	stay

Sentences

1. Stay away from the table.
2. He's able to maintain a state of tranquility even in difficult times.
3. Their aim is to change and improve our way of life.
4. Who would you say are your eight favorite authors?
5. My main concern today is finding someone to take care of the baby.

/e/ aim

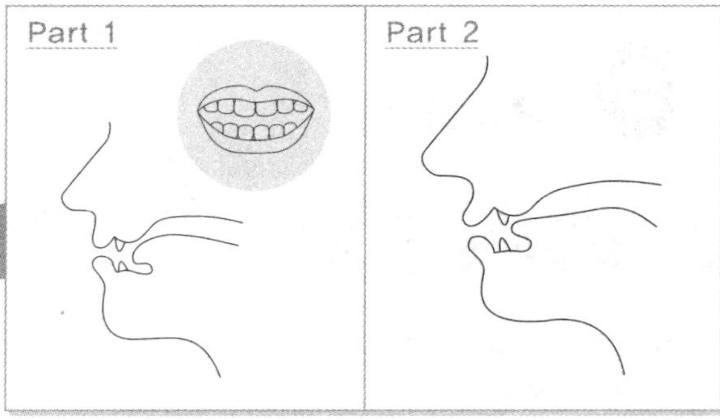

● Day 2

To make the /e/ sound, open your mouth and spread your lips a little. Place your tongue, with the sides slightly curled upward, near the front of your mouth. Begin vibrating your vocal cords and pull the front of your tongue closer to the top of your mouth, ending in an /i/ sound. When you make this sound, your face and jaw should be tense. Make the transition so quickly that you pronounce the sound as one syllable.

Words

INITIAL	MEDIAL	FINAL
aim	**fa**mous	pay
acres	**may**be	gray
aids	plane	clay
agent	straight	**yes**terday
eight	break	May

Sentences

1. The day before yesterday was Tuesday.
2. The United States Army dropped Agent Orange over six million acres of land.
3. Maybe we ate breakfast too late.
4. Straight people can get AIDS just as easily as gay people.
5. We used a gray-colored clay to make our ceramics.

/ə/ alone

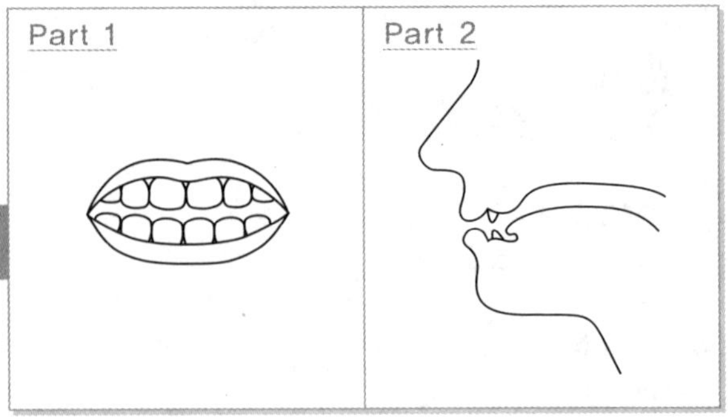

To make the /ə/ sound, open your mouth just a little. Rest your tongue in the center of your mouth. When you make this sound, your face and jaw should be relaxed. Put your hand on your diaphragm and push until a grunt escapes. Don't move your jaw, tongue, or lips. Just allow the sound to flow past your vocal cords.

Words

INITIAL	MEDIAL	FINAL
a**lone**	done	Cali**for**nia
a**mount**	sun	**Chi**na
a**head**	com**plete**	**Ma**ma
ob**serve**	what	A**las**ka
un**less**	**some**one	**Ca**nada

Sentences

1. A great amount of energy comes from the sun.
2. China has done well in educating its population.
3. I won't know what's going on unless someone tells me.
4. Not all parts of Canada observe Daylight Savings Time.
5. I wanted to take a trip from California to Alaska alone.

/e/ & /ə/ ape-up

Review

Practice distinguishing between the /e/ and /ə/ sounds. Remember that the /e/ sound is formed with your lips spread and your face and jaw tight while the /ə/ sound is formed with your mouth open only slightly and your face and jaw relaxed.

Words

INITIAL	MEDIAL	FINAL
ape - up	blade - blood	they - the
ace - us	game - gum	hey - huh
	gain - gun	
	rain - run	
	sane - son	

Sentences

1. She made up an excuse for being late.
2. Huh? What did you say?
3. I want to make sure we don't run out of cups.
4. The citizens of this nation are not allowed to carry guns.
5. I'm doing research to gain a better understanding of our country's history.

/ər/ earn

To make the /ər/ sound, form the shape of the /ə/ sound with your mouth. Vibrate your vocal cords and immediately press the sides of your tongue against your back molar teeth, forming the /r/ sound. Make the vowel sound very short.

Words

INITIAL	MEDIAL	FINAL
earn	**cir**cle	**wa**ter
earlier	**go**vernment	**or**der
earliest	heard	were
urban	re**turn**	**whe**ther
urged	**i**ron	**win**ter

Sentences

1. The earliest reports of crop circles date back to the ninth century.
2. My sister urged me to get the girl's number.
3. In order to earn points, your answers must be correct.
4. Let's return to the matter we were talking about earlier.
5. I don't know whether to travel in the winter or the summer.

/U/ cook

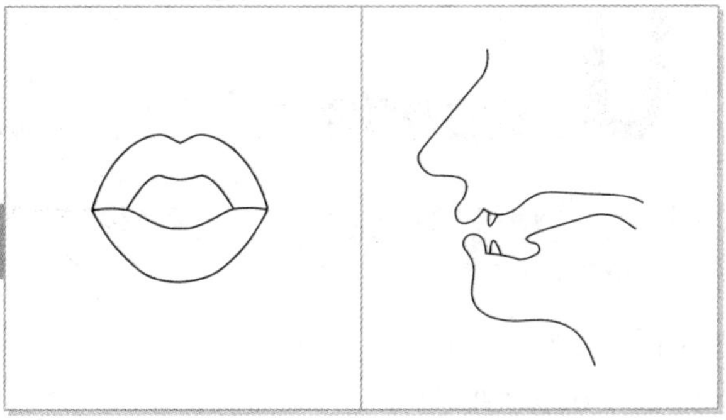

Day 1

To make the /U/ sound, round your lips tightly. Pull your tongue high up in the back of your mouth. Then, keeping the same position with your tongue, relax your face and jaw.

Words

INITIAL	MEDIAL		FINAL
none	cook	**coo**kies	*none*
	wool	**pu**tting	
	would	**woul**dn't	
	wooden	**neigh**borhood	
	football	Ju**ly**	

Sentences

1. Would you like me to cook dinner for you tonight?
2. He pulled the wool over everyone's eyes.
3. The football coach is putting too much pressure on me.
4. I wouldn't recommend moving to that neighborhood.
5. She stirred the cookie dough with a wooden spoon.

/U/ woods

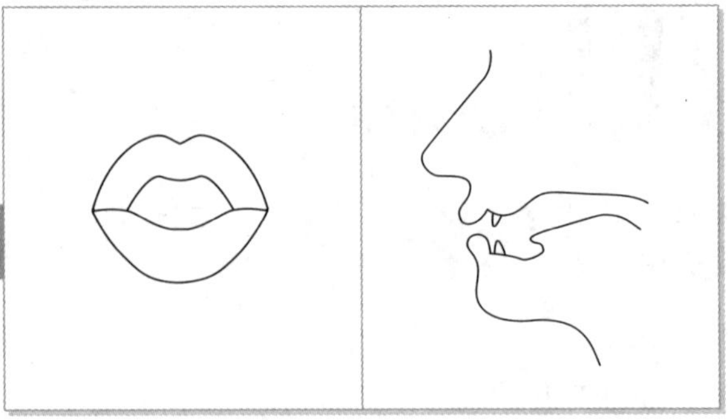

● Day 2

To make the /U/ sound, round your lips tightly. Pull your tongue high up in the back of your mouth. Then, keeping the same position with your tongue, relax your face and jaw.

Words

INITIAL	MEDIAL		FINAL
none	woods	**out**look	*none*
	output	**ful**ly	
	cooking	**bu**llet	
	childhood	**pul**monary	
	Brooklyn	**pu**lling	

Sentences

1. I spent much of my childhood playing in the woods.
2. He had never fully realized how much he missed his home in Brooklyn.
3. She suffered from a pulmonary bullet wound.
4. The outlook is grim for North Korea's food output.
5. Cooking crabs is difficult because it requires pulling off their shells.

/u/ food

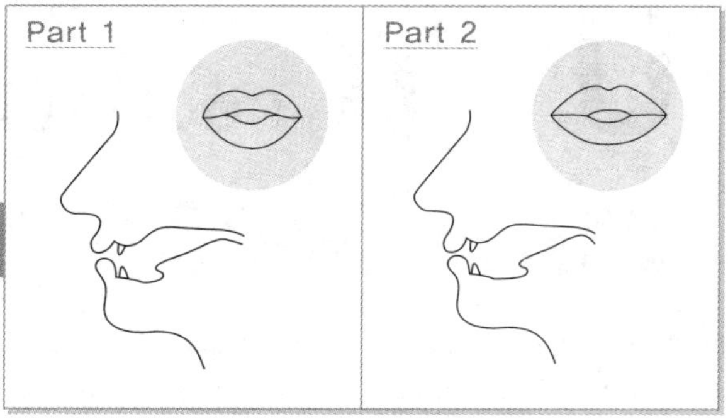

To make the /u/ sound, form the shape of the /U/ sound with your mouth, but do not relax your face and jaw. Begin vibrating your vocal cords and pull your tongue back even further while tightening your lips even more.

Words	INITIAL	MEDIAL	FINAL
	none	food	two
		soon	who
		whose	you
		moon	knew
		groups	blue

Sentences

1. Do you like Korean food?
2. Whose blue shoes are those?
3. My favorite band will be releasing two new CDs soon.
4. There are some people who believe the moon landing was an illusion.
5. I never knew that Tucson could be so cool.

/U/ & /u/ soot-suit

Review

Practice distinguishing between the /U/ and /u/ sounds. Remember that the formation of the mouth is similar for these two sounds. /U/ is the sound formed with a relaxed face and jaw. /u/ is the sound formed with tight lips.

Words

INITIAL	MEDIAL		FINAL
none	soot - suit	wood - wooed	*none*
	could - cooed	stood - stewed	
	hood - who'd	look - Luke	

Sentences

1. I'm going to look for a new suit this evening.
2. You should not bring pets to the pool.
3. Luke, could you do me a favor?
4. I am so full. The food was good.
5. You can't fool me by hiding under your hood.

/yu/ unit

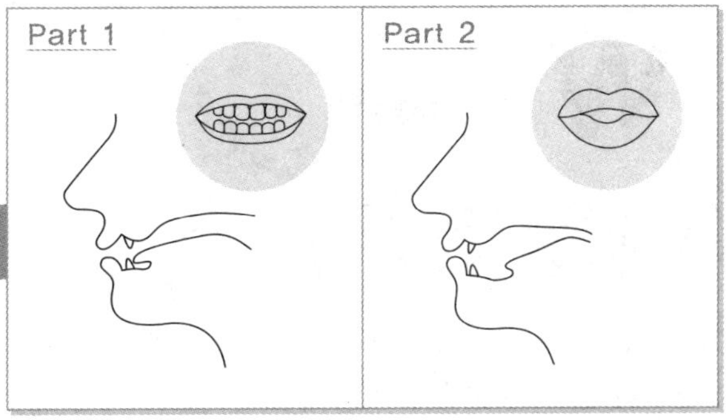

To make the /yu/ sound, open your mouth a little and pull your lips back into a tight smile. Raise the sides of your tongue toward the top of your mouth as high as you can without touching it. Allow the tip of your tongue to touch your lower teeth. Vibrate your vocal cords and immediately pull your tongue high up in the back of your mouth and tighten your lips, forming the /u/ sound.

Words

INITIAL	MEDIAL	FINAL
unit	**beau**ty	few
union	**hu**man	view
useful	**fu**ture	re**view**
you've	co**mmu**nity	**in**terview
you'll	**vol**ume	**ar**gue

Sentences

1. Do you know how to use chopsticks?
2. You live in a beautiful community.
3. I have an interview in just a few minutes.
4. The dollar is the monetary unit of the United States.
5. You'll need to review this lesson sometime in the future.

/W/ warm

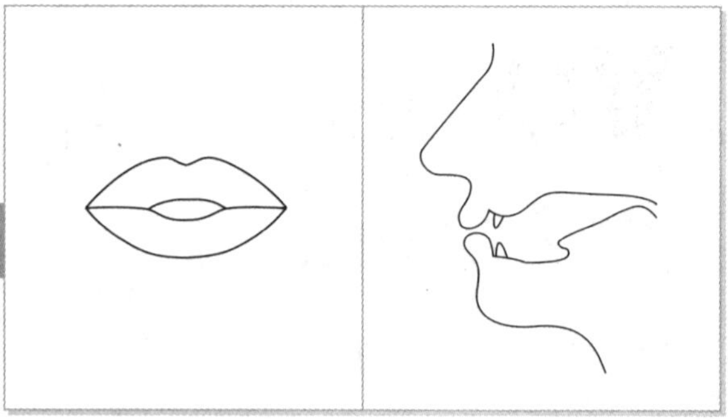

● Day 1

To make the /w/ sound, round your lips tightly until they are almost closed, as if you are going to whistle. Vibrate your vocal cords for a very short sound. Then open your lips widely to pronounce the next sound in the word.

Words

INITIAL	MEDIAL	FINAL
warm	**for**ward	*none*
war	swim	
ward	twice	
woman's	twelve	
wound	**a**nyway	

Sentences

1. I usually swim once or twice a week.
2. Anyway, I won't be home before twelve.
3. I look forward to a warm welcome when I get home.
4. In this ward, we care for patients with open wounds and burns.
5. I just finished a book about one woman's bravery during World War II.

/W/ wolf

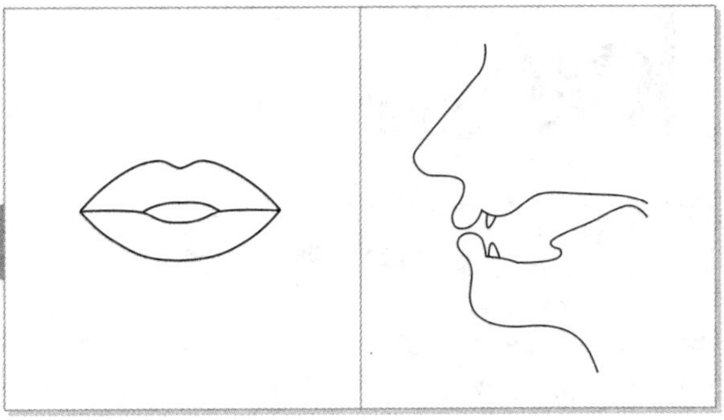

● Day 2

To make the /w/ sound, round your lips tightly until they are almost closed, as if you are going to whistle. Vibrate your vocal cords for a very short sound. Then open your lips widely to pronounce the next sound in the word.

Words	INITIAL	MEDIAL	FINAL
	wolf	**twen**ty	*none*
	warmth	sweet	
	wore	**swi**mming	
	warned	**high**way	
	wounded	**Ed**ward	

Sentences

1. Edward was wounded and became a prisoner of war.
2. We bought twenty pounds of sweet potatoes for Thanksgiving dinner.
3. I wore my winter jacket for extra warmth.
4. He warned the children to stay away from the swimming pool.
5. I was driving along the highway when I saw a gray wolf.

/kw/ quietly

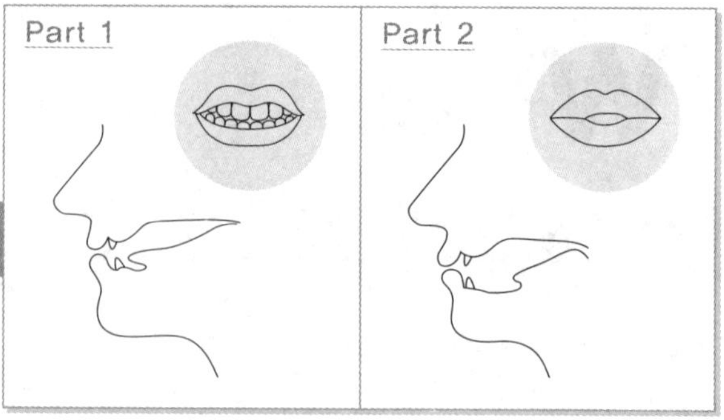

● Day 1

The letters *qu* are pronounced as /kw/. Form the /k/ sound with your mouth. As you release the /k/, immediately round your lips tightly, forming the /w/ sound.

Words

INITIAL	MEDIAL	FINAL
quietly	**li**quid	*none*
quoted	e**quip**ment	
questioned	**fre**quently	
questio**nnaire**	**e**qually	
qualifi**ca**tion	e**qua**tor	

Sentences

1. She snuck out quietly at a quarter to three.
2. The equipment in our lab frequently fails.
3. I questioned each person in the interview equally.
4. Fill out this questionnaire to test your knowledge of liquids, solids and gases.
5. He quoted from Mark Twain's book *Following the Equator.*

/kw/ quiet

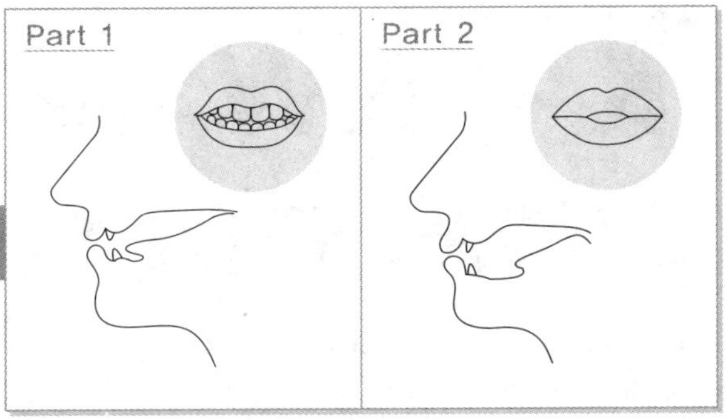

Day 2

The letters *qu* are pronounced as /kw/. Form the /k/ sound with your mouth. As you release the /k/, immediately round your lips tightly, forming the /w/ sound.

Words	INITIAL	MEDIAL	FINAL
	quiet	re**quire**	*none*
	questions	re**quest**	
	quantity	e**qui**valent	
	qualities	e**quipped**	
	qualified	**se**quence	

Sentences

1. I have some questions about the quadratic equations quiz.
2. Quality is more important than quantity.
3. I'm not qualified or equipped to do this job well.
4. Which qualities would you require in a mate?
5. I'd like to request the following sequence of events.

/k/ & /kw/ kick-quick

● Review

Practice distinguishing between the /k/ and /kw/ sounds. When making the /kw/ sound, remember to immediately tighten your lips after making the /k/ sound so that the /w/ sound is formed.

Words

INITIAL		MEDIAL	FINAL
kick - quick	kill - quill	*none*	*none*
cake - quake	kite - quite		
coral - **quarr**el	coat - quote		
keen - queen	kilt - quilt		
kale - quail	courts - quartz		

Sentences

1. The quake killed 3,000 people across the state.
2. Let's take a quick break.
3. I'm not quite ready to quit smoking.
4. My cousin and I quarreled over the last piece of cake.
5. I'll make the quilt to fit on a queen-sized bed.

LEVEL 4

/t/ & /θ/ true-threw

Review

Practice distinguishing between the /t/ and /θ/ sounds. Remember that the /t/ sound is formed with the tip of your tongue against the ridge that is behind your upper front teeth while the /θ/ sound is formed with the tip of your tongue between your teeth.

Words	INITIAL	MEDIAL	FINAL
	true - threw	**ea**ter - **e**ther	heat - heath
	taught - thought	**nu**tting - **no**thing	tent - tenth
	tank - thank	**pla**ting - **play**thing	wit - with
	torn - thorn	forts - fourths	debt - death
	tie - thigh	fates - faiths	clot - cloth

Sentences

1. Thank you for coming with me to the doctor.
2. I was taught that it's the thought that counts.
3. This is the tenth time I've had to rethread this needle.
4. My company threw an extravagant black-tie ball on New Year's Eve.
5. It is true that death may come at any time.

/d/ & /ð/ day-they

● Review

Practice distinguishing between the /d/ and /ð/ sounds. Remember that the /d/ sound is formed with the tip of your tongue along the ridge that is behind your upper front teeth while the /ð/ sound is formed with the tip of your tongue between your teeth.

Words

INITIAL	MEDIAL	FINAL
day - they	**ri**ding - **wri**thing	tide - tithe
doze - those	**u**dder - **o**ther	laid - lathe
dough - though	**wor**dy - **wor**thy	seed - seethe
dare - their	**bla**dder - **bla**ther	sued - soothe
den - then	**hea**der - **hea**ther	read - wreathe

Sentences

1. I enjoy riding dirt bikes every now and then.
2. What other types of seeds do the birds like to eat?
3. Though it was a beautiful day, she wanted to stay home and read.
4. She daydreamed of a soothing stroll through fields of heather.
5. Those girls would dare to do anything.

-ed endings

● Review

Practice the -ed endings. Remember that the -ed ending can be pronounced in three ways--/t/, /d/ and /Id/.

Words	FINAL /t/	FINAL /d/	FINAL /Id/
	faced	be**lieved**	**no**ted
	ex**peri**enced	planned	**mel**ted
	pushed	ex**claimed**	**trea**ted
	ad**vanced**	in**volved**	su**ppor**ted
	laughed	saved	de**vo**ted

Sentences

1. I work at an experienced and skilled law firm devoted to estate planning.
2. I ordered a big bowl of chili covered with melted cheese.
3. She laughed and exclaimed, "You scared me!"
4. Planned Parenthood counsels women who are faced with unwanted pregnancies.
5. I was saved because my family loved and supported me.

/s/ & /z/ sue-zoo

Review

Practice distinguishing between the /s/ and /z/ sounds. Remember that the formation of the mouth is the same for both sounds. /s/ is the sound formed without vibrating your vocal cords. /z/ is the sound formed while vibrating your vocal cords.

Words

INITIAL	MEDIAL	FINAL
sue - zoo	**pri**ces - **pri**zes	vice - vies
sown - zone	**mu**scles - **mu**zzles	tense - tens
sipping - **zi**pping	**loo**sing - **lo**sing	false - falls
sapped - zapped	**la**ciest - **la**ziest	scarce - scares
sing - zing	**gra**cing - **gra**zing	race - raise

Sentences

1. We had to reduce our prices because we were losing business.
2. It just doesn't make any sense to me.
3. What scares you the most about going to graduate school?
4. Thank you for gracing us with your presence.
5. The muscles in my shoulders are very tense.

-S endings

Review

Practice the -s endings. Remember that the -s ending can be pronounced in three ways--/s/, /z/ and /Iz/.

Words	FINAL /s/	FINAL /z/	FINAL /Iz/
	re**marks**	rays	**lang**uages
	characte**ris**tics	**lay**ers	**co**lleges
	boats	stairs	**voi**ces
	moments	stems	**e**dges
	sports	claws	**i**mages

Sentences

1. Many dentists use x-rays to find cavities in their patients' teeth.
2. We are able to repair cars, trucks and boats.
3. The happiest moments of my life were spent playing sports with my brothers.
4. Linguists study the various characteristics of languages.
5. The president introduced representatives from several colleges and universities.

/p/ & /f/ pond-fond

● Review

Practice distinguishing between the /p/ and /f/ sounds. Remember that the /p/ sound is formed by a burst of air from your lips while the /f/ sound is formed using your upper teeth and lower lip.

Words

INITIAL	MEDIAL	FINAL
pond - fond	**co**py - **co**ffee	gulp - gulf
pride - fried	**pu**ppy - **pu**ffy	sheep - sheaf
pact - fact	**su**pper - **su**ffer	tip - tiff
port - fort	shipped - shift	snip - sniff
prance - France	de**pend** - de**fend**	whip - whiff

Sentences

1. Phil made a pact to meet his friend in France.
2. I promised to join my friend for coffee after supper.
3. Look at that farmer feeding his sheep.
4. I'm fond of tossing food to ducks at the pond.
5. Depend on your lawyer to defend your case and provide good advice.

/b/ & /v/ boat-vote

● Review

Practice distinguishing between the /b/ and /v/ sounds. Remember that the /b/ sound is formed by a burst of air from your lips while the /v/ sound is formed using your upper teeth and lower lip.

Words	INITIAL	MEDIAL	FINAL
	boat - vote	**cu**pboard - **co**vered	swab - suave
	bow - vow	**mar**ble - **mar**vel	dub - dove
	bowel - **vow**el	**sa**ber - **sa**vor	robe - rove
	bolt - volt	TB - TV	curb - curve
	bet - vet	lobes - loaves	verb - verve

Sentences

1. The President vows to veto the bill.
2. Leave three loaves of bread in the cupboard.
3. I believe you missed the boat on several important facts.
4. One bolt of lightning can carry over a million volts of electricity.
5. I can't help but marvel at the rapid development of biotechnology.

/l/ & /r/ lamp-ramp

Review

Practice distinguishing between the /l/ and /r/ sounds. Remember that the /l/ sound is formed using the tip of your tongue while the /r/ sound is formed using the sides of your tongue.

Words

INITIAL	MEDIAL	FINAL
lamp - ramp	**plea**sant - **pre**sent	roll - roar
lift - rift	climb - crime	mole - more
lush - rush	clue - crew	stole - store
loyal - **roy**al	clutch - crutch	goal - gore
long - wrong	fleas - freeze	foal - four

Sentences

1. I'm really sorry, but I'm a little rushed.
2. A rift developed between us after he stole my girlfriend.
3. You can buy a new lamp from the store on the corner.
4. Most people are more loyal to their friends than to their work.
5. The Royal Family will travel to Thailand next week.

/č/ & /š/ chop-shop

Review

Practice distinguishing between the /č/ and /š/ sounds. Remember that the /č/ sound is formed with the entire front of your tongue along the ridge that is behind your upper front teeth while the /š/ is the sound formed with the tip of your tongue pulled back slightly from the ridge that is behind your upper front teeth.

Words

INITIAL	MEDIAL	FINAL
chop - shop	**la**tches - **la**shes	catch - cash
cheese - she's	**cru**tches - **cru**shes	match - mash
choose - shoes	**lee**ches - **lea**shes	watch - wash
cheat - sheet	switched - swished	ditch - dish
cheap - sheep	**Ra**chel - **ra**cial	witch - wish

Sentences

1. She'd like to watch a show on a different channel.
2. That shop accepts only cash or checks.
3. I wish I had some cheddar cheese to put on this sandwich.
4. Rachel washed all the dishes for me after lunch.
5. I can't choose between the lamb chops and the mashed potatoes.

/ž/ genre

● Review

Review the /ž/ sound. Remember that the /ž/ sound is made by forming the shape of the /š/ sound with your mouth and vibrating your vocal cords.

Words

INITIAL	MEDIAL	FINAL
genre	**ver**sion	co**llage**
	measures	mi**rage**
	con**fu**sion	cor**sage**
	pro**vi**sion	ma**ssage**
	pre**ci**sion	beige

Sentences

1. The test measures one's level of extroversion and introversion.
2. The massage therapist did her work with precision.
3. The man pinned a corsage to her beige gown.
4. The mirage created some confusion in our group.
5. The latest version of the bill makes provision for reform.

/o/ owner

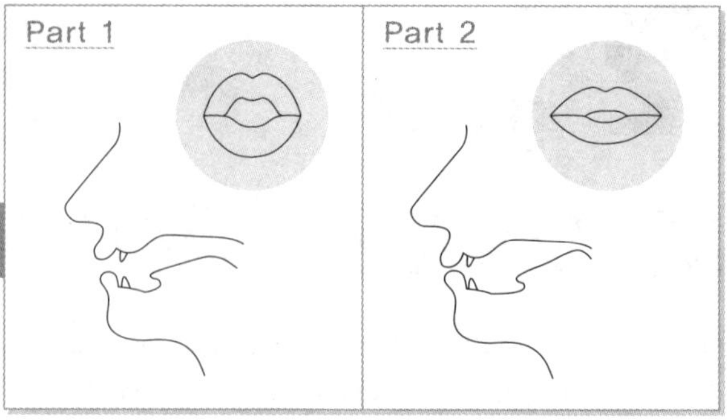

● Day 1

To make the /o/ sound, drop your jaw, making a round opening with your lips. The tip of your tongue should be drawn back a little and touching nothing. Begin vibrating your vocal cords and pull your tongue back even more while tightening your lips until you reach the /w/ position.

Words	INITIAL	MEDIAL	FINAL
	owner	hole	**fo**llow
	older	**low**er	no
	openly	post	**win**dow
	over**all**	gold	snow
	O**hi**o	hold	slow

Sentences

1. Don't be afraid to openly share your emotions with me.
2. I'm the owner of a doughnut shop in Ohio.
3. Sometimes the snow blows in through our windows.
4. Hormone levels may be lower in older people.
5. We followed the diggers, putting a post in each hole.

/o/ oldest

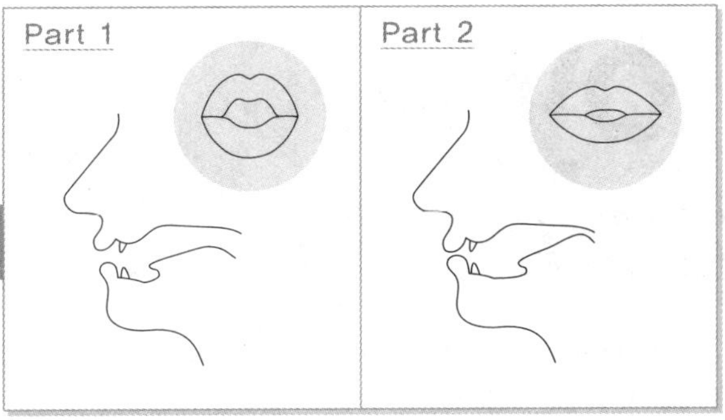

● Day 2

To make the /o/ sound, drop your jaw, making a round opening with your lips. The tip of your tongue should be drawn back a little and touching nothing. Begin vibrating your vocal cords and pull your tongue back even more while tightening your lips until you reach the /w/ position.

Words

INITIAL	MEDIAL	FINAL
oldest	**mo**ment	**ye**llow
over**come**	**bro**ken	**fe**llow
owned	stone	to**morr**ow
over**seas**	sold	flow
Owen	**close**ly	Chi**ca**go

Sentences

1. I once owned a home in Chicago.
2. This is the third time Owen has broken his nose.
3. At the moment, I have no motivation to keep trying.
4. She hung a yellow ribbon on the oak tree when her oldest son went to war.
5. Martin Luther King, Jr. and his fellow protestors sang “We Shall Overcome.”

/oy/ oil

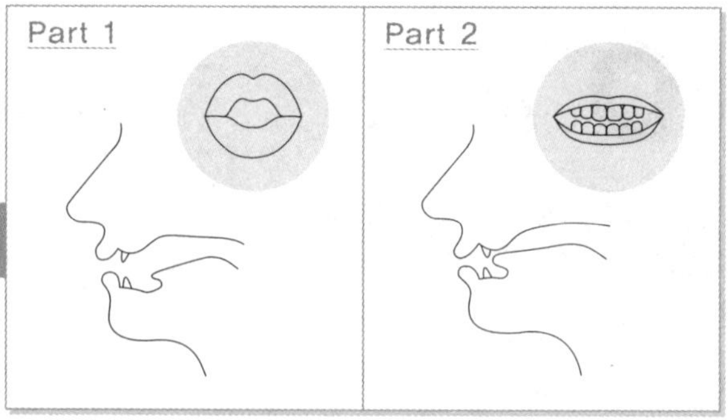

Day 1

To make the /oy/ sound, form the shape of the /o/ sound with your mouth. Begin vibrating your vocal cords and pull the front of your tongue closer to the top of your mouth, ending in an /i/ sound. Make the transition quickly so that you pronounce the sound as one syllable.

Words

INITIAL	MEDIAL	FINAL
oil	joint	em**ploy**
oily	em**ploy**ment	**con**voy
oil field	de**stroyed**	**cow**boy
oil well	a**void**	**a**lloy
oyster	a**ppoint**ment	Illi**nois**

Sentences

1. The two oil companies employed 5,000 people in their joint venture.
2. The convoy was destroyed on its way to the oil field.
3. Oily debris from nearby oil wells threatens the local oyster beds.
4. If you have a choice, try to avoid setting your appointment on Monday.
5. As a kid, I dreamed of leaving Illinois to become a cowboy.

/oy/ ointment

● Day 2

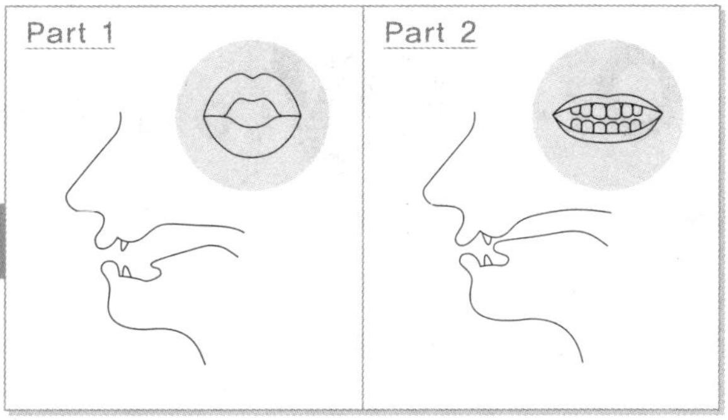

To make the /oy/ sound, form the shape of the /o/ sound with your mouth. Begin vibrating your vocal cords and pull the front of your tongue closer to the top of your mouth, ending in an /i/ sound. Make the transition quickly so that you pronounce the sound as one syllable.

Words

INITIAL	MEDIAL	FINAL
ointment	ap**poin**ted	**school**boy
oils	a**voi**ded	**en**voy
oiled	em**ployed**	de**stroy**
oil slick	**thy**roid	ploy
oil **tan**ker	De**troit**	a**nnoy**

Sentences

1. I read in *The Detroit News* that an oil tanker was destroyed.
2. Strong smelling oils and ointments annoy me.
3. The oil slick was avoided, thanks to the four scientists appointed to the project.
4. De-oiled lecithin can be employed in treating hyperthyroid conditions.
5. He was only a schoolboy, but he joined them on their dangerous voyage.

/o/ & /oy/ old-oiled

Review

Practice distinguishing between the /o/ and /oy/ sounds. When making the /oy/ sound, remember to pull the front of your tongue closer to the top of your mouth, ending in an /i/ sound.

Words	INITIAL	MEDIAL	FINAL
	old - oiled	knows - noise	beau - boy
		soul - soil	so - soy
		told - toiled	toe - toy
		loan - loin	row - Roy
		host - hoist	Joe - joy

Sentences

1. He's only a four-year-old boy.
2. I told Roy to put the soy sauce away.
3. It's a joy to watch children open their toys on Christmas Day.
4. Joe's only complaint about living in the city is all the noise.
5. We toiled in the hot sun, digging row after row in the rich, dark soil.

/ɔ/ audience

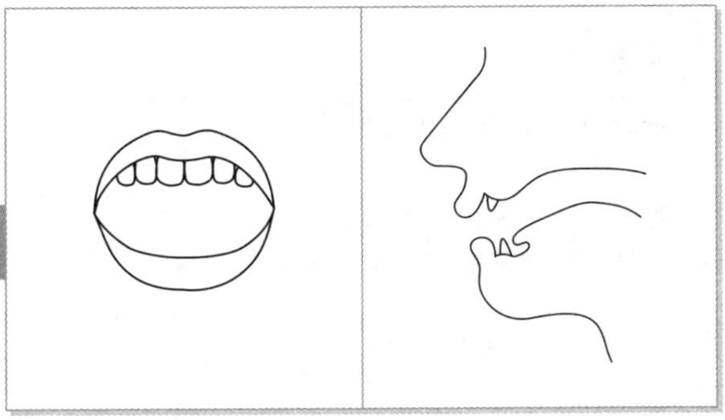

Day 1

To make the /ɔ/ sound, form the shape of the /a/ sound with your mouth, with your mouth opened wide and your jaw dropped. Then round your lips and pull your tongue back slightly before you vibrate your vocal cords.

Words

INITIAL	MEDIAL	FINAL
audience	gone	saw
al**ter**native	brought	straw
automobile	call	jaw
al**rea**dy	tall	thaw
auto**ma**tically	caught	**War**saw

Sentences

1. I saw no alternative but to call my parents for help.
2. Too many things have already gone wrong.
3. The piece by the Warsaw Philharmonic Orchestra brought the audience to its feet.
4. I have to drink with a straw because I broke my jaw in an automobile accident.
5. Because I am tall, people automatically assume I play basketball.

/ɔ/ autumn

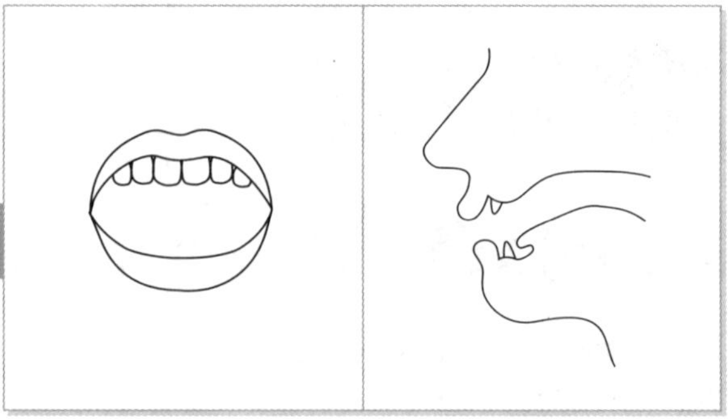

● Day 2

To make the /ɔ/ sound, form the shape of the /a/ sound with your mouth, with your mouth opened wide and your jaw dropped. Then round your lips and pull your tongue back slightly before you vibrate your vocal cords.

Words	INITIAL	MEDIAL	FINAL
	autumn	lost	flaw
	auto**ma**tic	salt	with**draw**
	authorized	broad	**bro**ther-in-law
	Au**stral**ia	be**long**	**son**-in-law
	August	**daugh**ter	**mo**ther-in-law

Sentences

1. My daughter and son-in-law got married last autumn.
2. We lost all of our belongings in a fire.
3. Does your brother-in-law live on Broad Street in Salt Lake City?
4. I authorized the automatic withdrawal of 100,000 won per month.
5. My mother-in-law will spend the month of August in Australia.

/O/ okay

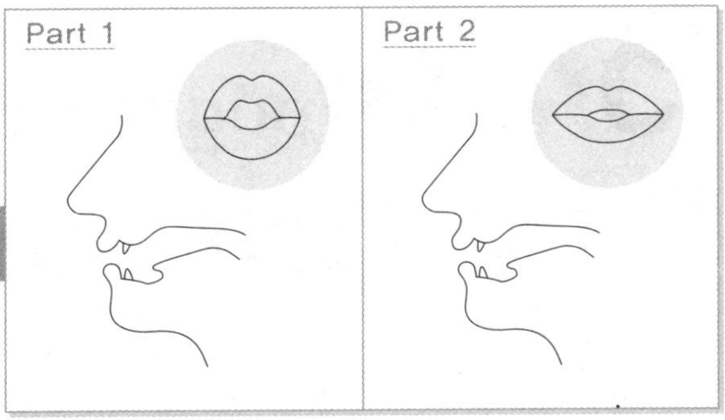

Review

Review the /o/ sound. Remember that the /o/ sound is made by dropping your jaw and making a round opening with your lips. The tip of your tongue should be drawn back a little and touching nothing. Begin vibrating your vocal cords and pull your tongue back even more while tightening your lips until you reach the /w/ position.

Words

INITIAL	MEDIAL	FINAL
o**kay**	whole	**bu**ffalo
opened	**slow**ly	pi**a**no
owners	su**ppose**	**sha**dow
ownership	wrote	**arr**ow
over**whel**ming	clothes	**ho**llow

Sentences

1. Okay. I suppose I can go with you.
2. Reading *The Chosen* opened my eyes to a whole new world.
3. I started playing the piano when I was only three years old.
4. American buffalo have slowly become mostly domesticated animals.
5. I wrote a note to the owners of the inn, thanking them for their service.

/ɔ/ & /o/ ought-oat

● Review

Practice distinguishing between the /ɔ/ and /o/ sounds. The /o/ sound is formed with lips more rounded and the tongue pulled back farther than when making the /ɔ/ sound.

Words	INITIAL	MEDIAL	FINAL
	ought - oat	bald - bold	slaw - slow
	awed - owed	chalk - choke	saw - sew
	off - oaf	hall - hole	law - low
	awe - oh	want - won't	gnaw - know
		walk - woke	jaw - Joe

Sentences

1. Maybe we ought to throw out the whole idea and start over.
2. Joe asked for coleslaw with his fried chicken.
3. He won't ever go bald.
4. I know she wants to take next Friday off.
5. The walk along the coast was awe-inspiring.

/or/ or

To make the /or/ sound, form the shape of the /o/ sound with your mouth. Vibrate your vocal cords and immediately press the sides of your tongue against the inside of your back molar teeth, forming the /r/ sound.

Words	INITIAL	MEDIAL	FINAL
	or	board	door
	orbit	corn	nor
	organized	form	**there**fore
	origin	born	score
	ordinary	**for**est	ex**plore**

Sentences

1. The board presented itself in an organized form.
2. Were you born before or after your sister?
3. We explored the theory to find out more about its origin.
4. She is neither ordinary nor extraordinary.
5. I smelled warm cornbread as I walked through the door.

/a/ opera

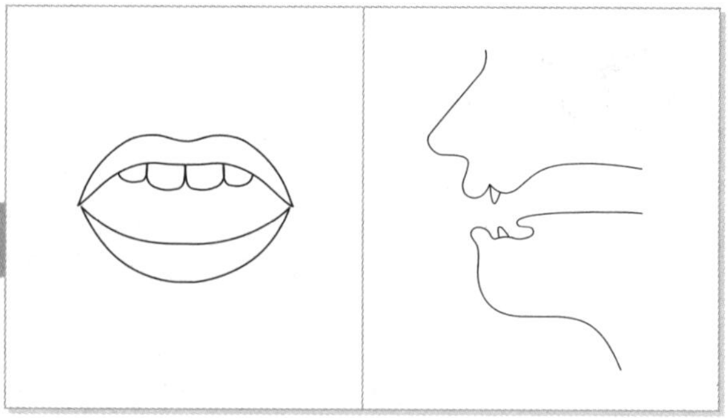

● Review

Review the /a/ sound. Remember that the /a/ sound is made by opening your mouth wide and dropping your jaw. Rest your tongue on the bottom of your mouth without touching your teeth. When you make this sound, your face and jaw should be relaxed.

Words

INITIAL	MEDIAL	FINAL
opera	**pro**blem	*none*
operate	stop	
oppor**tu**nities	lot	
operator	**so**lid	
oppo**si**tion	Tom	

Sentences

1. One possible solution to the problem is to operate.
2. Around the world, there is a solid opposition to poverty.
3. One-stop shopping centers can save you a lot of time.
4. I've had many opportunities to volunteer at the opera house.
5. Tom called the operator and got the number for the hospital.

/ay/ eye

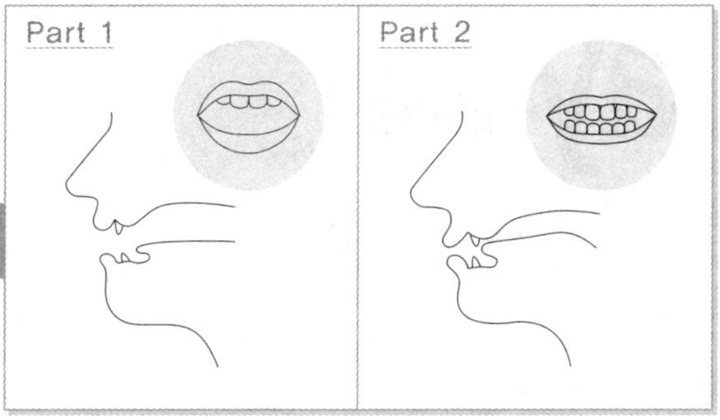

● Day 1

To make the /ay/ sound, form the shape of the /a/ sound with your mouth. Begin vibrating your vocal cords and raise the sides of your tongue toward the top of your mouth, ending in an /i/ sound. Make the transition quickly so that you pronounce the sound as one syllable.

Words

INITIAL	MEDIAL	FINAL
eye	**sci**ence	by
I'll	fight	dry
I'm	wide	why
ideally	wild	try
identified	slide	high

Sentences

1. By the way, I might not be free tomorrow.
2. Here, use some of my tissue to dry your eyes.
3. I'm going to try being a vegetarian for a while.
4. Biologists have identified the largest coral reef known to science.
5. I'll never understand why my sister and I always fight.

/ay/ island

Day 2

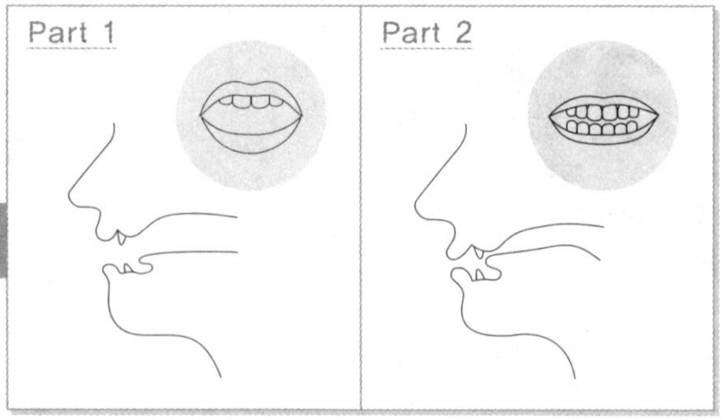

To make the /ay/ sound, form the shape of the /a/ sound with your mouth. Begin vibrating your vocal cords and raise the sides of your tongue toward the top of your mouth, ending in an /i/ sound. Make the transition quickly so that you pronounce the sound as one syllable.

Words	INITIAL	MEDIAL	FINAL
	island	white	pie
	identity	be**side**	lie
	isolated	**ti**ny	guy
	identical	mind	su**pply**
	ide**o**logy	type	cry

Sentences

1. Who was that nice guy sitting beside Ira?
2. I couldn't find a good excuse, so I lied.
3. Would you mind if I took a tiny bite of your sandwich?
4. Identical twins sometimes have trouble finding their own identities.
5. Would you like some raspberries on top of your white chocolate pie?

/a/ & /ay/ odd-I'd

Review

Practice distinguishing between the /a/ and /ay/ sounds. When making the /ay/ sound, remember to raise the sides of your tongue toward the top of your mouth, ending in an /i/ sound.

Words	INITIAL	MEDIAL	FINAL
	odd - I'd	blond - blind	*none*
		pop - pipe	
		hot - height	
		loss - lice	
		God - guide	

Sentences

1. I'd like to know more about God.
2. Osteoporosis can lead to a loss of height.
3. I help train guide dogs for the blind.
4. The hot water pipe broke and flooded the library.
5. He has spiky blond hair and an odd sense of humor.

/ayr/ ire

To make the /ayr/ sound, first make the /ay/ sound. Then immediately press the sides of your tongue against the inside of your back molar teeth, forming the /r/ sound.

Words	INITIAL	MEDIAL	FINAL
	ire	tired	higher
	Ireland	en**tire**ly	wire
		fireplace	en**tire**
		de**sired**	**em**pire
		hired	tire

Sentences

1. I hope to wire my entire house by myself.
2. The long flight from Ireland left him tired.
3. We want to build an entirely new fireplace.
4. I was hired to photograph the Empire State Building.
5. If your tire pressure is higher than recommended, your tires might blow out.

/æ/ actual

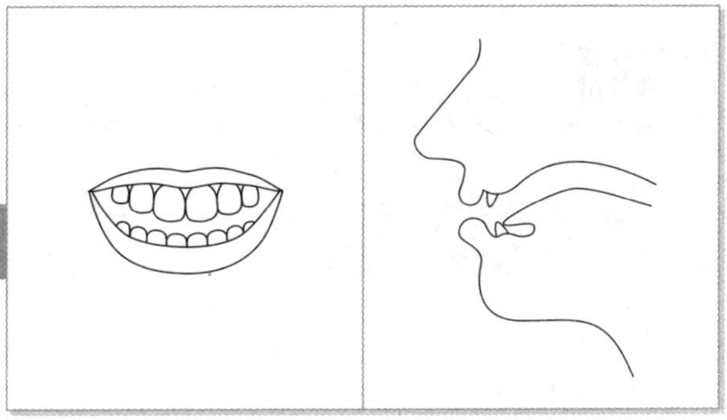

Review the /æ/ sound. Remember that the /æ/ sound is made by opening your mouth and spreading your lips. Lightly press the tip of your tongue against the back of your lower teeth. When you make this sound, your face and jaw should be relaxed.

Words	INITIAL	MEDIAL	FINAL
	actual	glad	*none*
	accurate	**ha**ppy	
	advertising	**ca**pital	
	absence	chance	
	Alice	**fas**ter	

Sentences

1. I'm glad you asked me to visit the capital with you.
2. Alice does fast and accurate work.
3. I'm happy I had the chance to take a leave of absence.
4. Can you speak faster in Spanish or in English?
5. We need to determine the actual cost of advertising in the magazine.

/aw/ outline

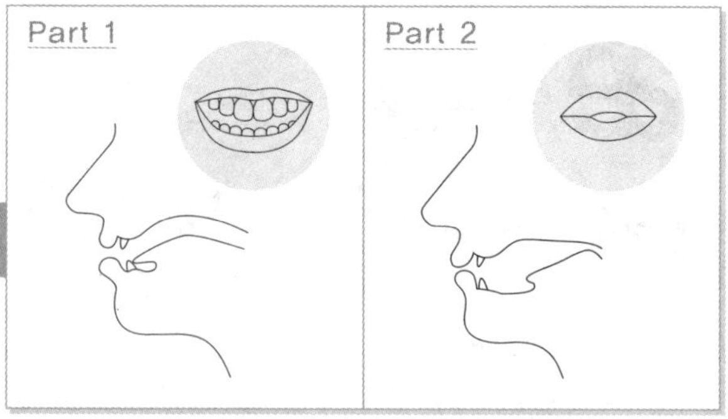

Day 1

To make the /aw/ sound, form the shape of the /æ/ sound with your mouth. Vibrate your vocal cords and immediately round your lips tightly, forming the /w/ sound, and release them to pronounce the next sound in the word. Make the transition quickly so that you pronounce the sound as one syllable.

Words

INITIAL	MEDIAL	FINAL
owl	round	how
oust	noun	brow
outline	brown	cow
out**stan**ding	pound	thou
outcomes	proud	a**llow**

Sentences

1. I only need one more James Brown CD to round out my collection.
2. She didn't know how else to help, so she dabbed his brow with a cool towel.
3. He pointed out how a clearer outline would bring better outcomes.
4. I was proud of my son's outstanding courage when he rescued the drowning man.
5. It takes a lot of food to feed a 1,000-pound cow.

/aw/ outdoor

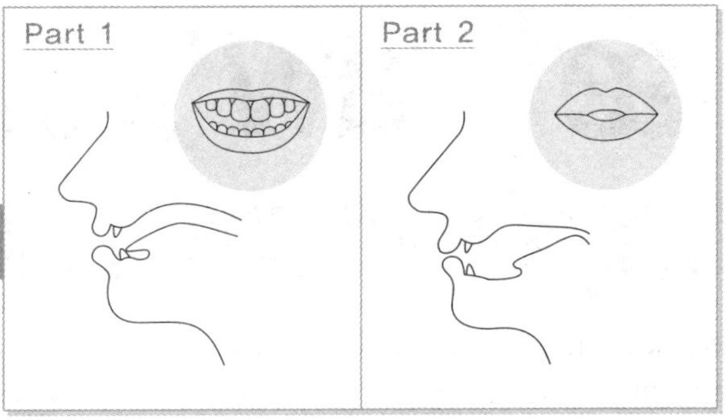

● Day 2

To make the /aw/ sound, form the shape of the /æ/ sound with your mouth. Vibrate your vocal cords and immediately round your lips tightly, forming the /w/ sound, and release them to pronounce the next sound in the word. Make the transition quickly so that you pronounce the sound as one syllable.

Words

INITIAL	MEDIAL	FINAL
ounce	doubt	plow
outdoor	a**ccount**	**some**how
outcome	a**loud**	**a**nyhow
outlined	**moun**tain	**eye**brow
outbreak	**com**pound	**Mos**cow

Sentences

1. I somehow doubt whether or not we'll achieve the desired outcome.
2. He didn't want to get dirty, but he sat down on the ground anyhow.
3. Have you heard any accounts of the flu outbreak in Moscow?
4. Please count down from 100 aloud.
5. She outlined the top of her eyebrow with an eyebrow pencil.

/æ/ & /aw/ at-out

Review

Practice distinguishing between the /æ/ and /aw/ sounds. When making the /aw/ sound, remember to round your lips tightly, ending in a /w/ sound.

Words

INITIAL	MEDIAL	FINAL
at - out	band - bound	*none*
Al - owl	can't - count	
	lad - loud	
	mass - mouse	
	sand - sound	

Sentences

1. She can't go out with you this afternoon.
2. I couldn't stand the loud noise coming from the band practice.
3. That sounds like a sad movie.
4. The mouse outsmarted the owl and ran away.
5. Counting grains of sand is a futile task.

/awr/ hours

To make the /awr/ sound, first make the /aw/ sound. Then immediately press the sides of your tongue against the inside of your back molar teeth, forming the /r/ sound.

Words	INITIAL	MEDIAL	FINAL
	hours	flowers	power
	our	towers	shower
	our**selves**	**power**ful	flour
	hourly	**power**less	**Ei**senhower
	hourglass	em**powered**	sour

Sentences

1. I spent hours researching President Eisenhower.
2. Sara felt empowered when she met her hourly goals.
3. The soprano was showered with flowers after her powerful finale.
4. I bought some flour to make our traditional sour cream cake.
5. David stared at the powerful giant towering above him.

/ɛ/ & /e/ edge-age

Review

Practice distinguishing between the /ɛ/ and /e/ sounds. Remember that the formation of the mouth is similar for these two sounds. They both begin with your mouth open, lips slightly spread, and tongue, slightly curled, near the front of your mouth. When making the /e/ sound, finish the sound by pulling the front of your tongue closer to the top of your mouth, ending in an /i/ sound.

Words

INITIAL	MEDIAL	FINAL
edge - age	wet - wait	*none*
Ed - aid	pen - pain	
L - ail	bell - bail	
M - aim	west - waste	
S - ace	debt - date	

Sentences

1. My aim is to ace my entrance exam.
2. Ed went into debt after losing his savings in a bet.
3. I waited for my date at the west entrance of the mall.
4. Everyone got wet as we bailed water over the edge of the boat.
5. Does pain help make us better individuals?

/I/ & /i/ itch-each

Review

Practice distinguishing between the /I/ and /i/ sounds. Remember that the formation of the mouth is similar for these two sounds. /I/ is the sound formed with a relaxed face and jaw. /i/ is the sound formed with a tense face and jaw and the tongue pulled a little closer to the top of the mouth.

Words

INITIAL	MEDIAL	FINAL
itch - each	mitt - meat	*none*
is - ease	his - he's	
it - eat	slip - sleep	
ill - eel	fill - feel	
	Tim - team	

Sentences

1. Eat it. It will help you feel better.
2. Is there anything that can ease my itch?
3. Tim treated his team to a meat loaf dinner.
4. She slipped warm mittens on her chilly fingers.
5. He's feeling ill, so he's going to sleep.

/æ/ & /a/ add-odd

● Review

Practice distinguishing between the /æ/ and /a/ sounds. Remember that the /æ/ sound is formed with your lips spread and your tongue resting against the back of your lower teeth while the /a/ sound is formed with your jaw dropped and your tongue not touching your bottom teeth.

Words

INITIAL	MEDIAL	FINAL
add - odd	pat - pot	*none*
ax - ox	stack - stock	
an - on	black - block	
apt - opt	shack - shock	
active - **oc**tave	**ma**ddest - **mo**dest	

Sentences

1. Pat is active in an online organization called MoveOn.org.
2. Add those boxes to the stack in the stockroom.
3. There's something odd about the frosting on that cake.
4. I opted to wear a modest black dress.
5. Halfway down the block, you'll see an old shack.

/ə/ & /ɔ/ done-dawn

● Review

Practice distinguishing between the /ə/ and /ɔ/ sounds. Remember that the /ə/ sound is formed with a completely relaxed face and jaw while the /ɔ/ sound is formed with the jaw slightly dropped and the lips rounded.

Words	INITIAL	MEDIAL	FINAL
	a - awe	done - dawn	*none*
		but - bought	
		lunch - launch	
		hunt - haunt	
		flood - flawed	

Sentences

1. By dawn, the rain had flooded the city.
2. The movie haunted me long after I saw it.
3. He bought lunch for everyone in the office but me.
4. I'm singing "Nothing but a Breeze" for my audition.
5. The launch was postponed after the discovery of flawed wiring in the space shuttle.

/U/ & /u/ could-cooed

● Review

Practice distinguishing between the /U/ and /u/ sounds. Remember that the formation of the mouth is similar for these two sounds. /U/ is the sound formed with a relaxed face and jaw. /u/ is the sound formed with tight lips and ending in the /w/ position.

Words

INITIAL	MEDIAL		FINAL
none	could - cooed	good - gooed	*none*
	hood - who'd	should - shooed	
	stood - stewed	wood - wooed	

Sentences

1. Should I wear a swimming suit in the pool?
2. You did a good job of choosing your husband.
3. Jenny stood on the roof and looked at the moon.
4. Could you call me back this afternoon?
5. You shouldn't talk with your mouth full of food.

You Too Can Speak English
Pronunciation Guide

LEVEL 5

Characters

• Me

My name is Kim Hyunmin.
I am 25 years old.
I am a university student studying guitar performance.

• My mom

This is my mom. She is 53 years old.
She is a wise woman.

• Sumi

This is my girlfriend, Sumi.
She is 27 years old.
I love her.

• Youngjin

This is my best friend, Lee Youngjin.
He is 25 years old.
We first met in high school.

• Kate

This is my English teacher, Kate Gallagher.
She is 29 years old.
She is from Ireland.

• Hyunjoon

This is my brother, Kim Hyunjoon.
He is 23 years old.
He is incorrigible.

• Professor Bak

This is Professor Bak.
He is 56 years old.
He is my advisor and teaches many of my classes.

• My neighbors

These are my neighbors, Hong Jaebaek and his daughter, Mina.
Mr. Hong is 33, and his daughter is 7.
They live downstairs in our building.

You Too Can Speak English

Week · 1 /p/, /f/, /b/, /v/

DAY 1 AN ECLIPSE

- eclipse
- happened
- roof
- flowers
- disappear
- reappear
- neighbor
- vegetables
- beautiful

Tonight, while I was watering the vegetables and flowers that grow on our roof, a man walked up the stairs with his little girl.

"Hello," I said.

"Hello," he replied. "Do you mind if we watch the eclipse from here?"

"Go ahead," I said.

We stood and watched the moon disappear and then reappear again.
It was beautiful.

"By the way, my name is Hong Jaebaek," the man said. "I live downstairs. This is my daughter, Mina."

"Nice to meet you, Mr. Hong," I said. "You too, Mina. I'm Kim Hyunmin."

That is how I happened to meet my neighbor.

DAY 2 PLANNING

- pizza
- Europe
- plan
- beyond
- broke
- begging
- delivery
- travel
- break

Today, my friend Youngjin talked to me about a plan he has.

"Let's travel somewhere over winter break," he said.

"Where do you want to go?" I asked.

"Europe would be cool. Or, you know, ever since I saw *The Lord of the Rings*, I've wanted to go to New Zealand."

"How are you going to pay for that?" I asked.
"You're broke."

"Maybe I could get a job as a pizza delivery man," he said. "Or I could just ask my mom. I am not beyond begging, you know."

DAY 3 MY ENGLISH TEACHER

• after	• wardrobe	• visiting
• spent	• believed	• level
• book	• copy	• gave

I take English classes at SDA Language School. I am in Level Five. This term, I am also taking a religion class from Kate Gallagher.

Tonight, I spent some time visiting with her after class. I asked her what kind of God she believed in.

"If I gave you an English book to read, would you read it?" she asked me.

"I'd try," I said.

So she gave me a copy of *The Lion, the Witch, and the Wardrobe.*

"I believe God is like a lion," she said. "Read it, and you'll understand what I mean."

DAY 4 THE SAUNA

• positioned	• laughed	• bunch
• stepped	• outfits	• uncomfortable
• pausing	• covered	• bravely

Today I went to the sauna. When I stepped into the salt room, I saw that it was very crowded. It was full of ladies wearing pink sauna outfits. I felt a little uncomfortable.

An older lady looked up at me pausing at the door. "What are you afraid of? A bunch of women?" she asked.

Everyone laughed.

"No," I said bravely. "I'm not afraid."

Even so, I positioned myself in the corner and covered my head with a towel.

DAY 5 LONG UNDERWEAR

• poor	• blood	• drive
• per	• besides	• serving
• first-aid	• November	• volunteering

I've been volunteering with the Red Cross since I was in high school. About a year ago, they gave me a job. Besides blood drives and first-aid courses, the Red Cross is also involved in many projects serving the poor. Right now, we are planning a long underwear drive for November. We'll collect long underwear and ship it to North Korea for the winter.

My mom is really excited about this project. Every time she sees long underwear on sale, she buys ten pairs.

"Look!" she told me today. "Only three thousand won per pair!"

Week·2 /t/, /d/, /θ/, /ð/

DAY 1 RAMYEON NOODLES

• street	• between	• behind
• chopsticks	• forgotten	• breakfast
• water	• toward	• noodles

Today, I didn't eat breakfast before leaving home, so by the time my first class was finished, I was really hungry. Between classes, I ran to the convenience store down the street and bought a bowl of *ramyeon* noodles. I put some hot water in the bowl and walked back toward the school.

When I arrived, my noodles were ready to eat. Suddenly, I realized that I had forgotten to pick up chopsticks at the convenience store.

I found an empty classroom and snuck inside. I closed and locked the door behind me.

Then I ate the noodles with my fingers.

DAY 2 SLEEPING

• fidget	• middle	• they're
• notebook	• drooled	• gather
• thought	• theory	• further

I fell asleep in the middle of music theory class today. My head kept drooping further and further until it landed on my desk. I drooled a little on my notebook.

When class was over, Professor Bak patted me on the arm. "I gather you haven't been sleeping much lately," he said.

"Sorry," I said. "I thought your lecture really was interesting."

"Don't worry," he said. "I realized a long time ago that when students are bored, they fidget and talk. They only fall asleep when they're really tired."

DAY 3 A REWARD

- entertainment
- spend
- worth
- cost
- reward
- think
- studying
- decided
- rhythms

I've been studying so hard this week that I decided to reward myself. I bought two tickets for the Kang Saneh concert--one for me and one for my girlfriend, Sumi.

The tickets cost me a full week's pay. I don't usually spend so much money on entertainment, but for Kang Saneh, it's worth it. I will enjoy it because I think his lyrics are meaningful and his songs have cool rhythms. Plus, he plays the guitar pretty well. Sumi will enjoy it because she thinks he's good-looking.

DAY 4 MASS

- hit
- thine
- throat
- talked
- ducked
- sympathy
- directly
- deliver
- Catholic

My mother is Catholic. I don't usually go to mass with her, but last Sunday, she talked me into going.

I did my best to pay attention. Then, before communion, we were saying The Lord's Prayer. I didn't realize that everyone paused after the line "deliver us from evil."

"For thine...!" I said loudly.

I ducked my head as the priest cleared his throat and looked directly at me. My mother did not give me any sympathy. In fact, she hit me on the arm.

DAY 5 NECKTIES

- recital
- neckties
- station
- according
- record
- though
- dressing
- grandfather
- clothing

Sumi and I went shopping for neckties today. I have a guitar recital next week, so I need to wear something nice.

I always take Sumi with me when I shop for clothing. According to her, when I shop by myself, I end up dressing like her grandfather. For the record, I think her grandfather is awesome.

We went to five very expensive shops, but we couldn't agree on a tie. Then I saw one in the subway station--brown with blue stripes. It was only 4,000 won. Sumi allowed me to buy it, even though it was a little ugly.

Week·3 /g/, /k/, /ks/, /gz/

DAY ❶ FROGS

- plagues
- drag
- again
- Kate's
- talking
- tricky
- frogs
- kept
- class

Tonight in Kate's religion class, we studied the Bible story of the plagues in Egypt. There were many difficult words, but I kept mispronouncing the simplest one--*frogs*. It's tricky.

All the way home on the bus, I stared out the window and thought about the word. Fff-raw-gzzz. I tried to get my mouth to wrap around it. I tried to drag out each sound. Fff-raw-gzzz. Over and over again. Fff-raw-gzzz.

Suddenly, I realized that I was talking out loud.

DAY ❷ CLEANING

- signal
- grown
- plug
- cleaning
- electrical
- sink
- extremely
- explanation
- rugs

When my mom starts cleaning the house like crazy, it's a signal that she is extremely angry. I came home today to find her wiping down the electrical outlets. The rugs looked like they had been beaten within an inch of their lives.

At first, I didn't say anything. I finally approached her as she was yanking the plug out of the bathroom sink.

"Who's in trouble this time?" I asked.

"Your brother. I don't want to talk about it."

"Okay," I said and left her to her drains. Having grown up with my brother, I needed no explanation.

DAY 3 USB DRIVES

- forgot
- guess
- organize
- week
- scales
- covered
- exhausted
- because
- index

Today, I forgot my USB drive at work. I do that at least once a week. I'm in the middle of writing a research paper on the variety of scales used in music. When I got home, I couldn't work on my paper because all of my information was on the USB drive.

I guess I could organize my index cards covered with notes. But to tell you the truth, I'm exhausted. The forgotten drive means I can go to bed early. Organizing can wait until tomorrow.

DAY 4 BAKLAVA

- Greek
- agree
- great
- baklava
- took
- sixteen
- mixture
- existence
- pigs

Tonight I went out with Kate and some students from our religion class. Kate took us to a Greek restaurant for dessert. She wanted us to try baklava. I didn't know what baklava was, so I looked it up online last night. I found out that it's a pastry filled with a mixture of nuts and honey.

Altogether, we ordered SIXTEEN servings of baklava. It was great. We ate like pigs.
I ate so much that I felt a little dizzy afterward.
Kate says that baklava is the best dessert in existence. I agree.

DAY 5 MY RECITAL

• greatest	• Korean	• make
• program	• because	• longer
• golden	• guitar	• angst

I had a recital tonight with some other guitar majors and our professor. For the final piece in the program, I played a duet with Professor Bak. We played a traditional Korean song--"Arirang." After a few moments, everyone in the audience started to sing along.

It was hard to hear the guitar because the people were singing, but I was not annoyed. I felt like the spotlight was no longer on me but on all the joy and angst that make up our history as a people. It was a golden moment--one of the greatest of my life.

Week 4 /m/, /n/, /ŋ/

DAY 1 FIRST DAY

- March
- nineteen
- handkerchief
- myself
- parents
- running
- students
- nose
- carrying

Today I found a picture of myself on my first day of school. That was nineteen years ago this March.

My parents and I were at the school entrance. My mom held on tightly to my hand. Students were running around the schoolyard behind us. I was carrying my new white indoor shoes, and there was a handkerchief in my front pocket. I always seemed to have a runny nose. My backpack was still empty.

That was a long time ago.

DAY 2 NOEL

- noel
- note
- young
- along
- listening
- song
- hum
- headphones
- king

While I was riding the subway today, a young man next to me was listening to music on his MP3 player. I could hear the song. It was "The First Noel."

When the chorus came, he started to sing. He thought he was singing quietly, but with his headphones on, he didn't realize how loud he was. "Noel, Noel, Noel, Noel." He squeaked on the high note. "Born is the King of Israel."

On the second verse, I started to hum along.

DAY ❸ CHRISTMAS DECORATIONS

- Christmas
- decorations
- home
- tonight
- almost
- wanted
- hanging
- candy
- Santa

I got home late from work tonight. I saw Mr. Hong and Mina on the stairs. Mina had a candy cane hanging from her mouth. Mr. Hong was wearing a Santa hat.

"Well, hello," I said.

"It's almost Christmas," Mina said.

"What are you doing out so late?" I asked.

"Mina wanted some Christmas decorations," Mr. Hong said, "so we went to Homeplus and bought some."

"But it's 11:30 at night," I said.

"Well, it *is* almost Christmas," he replied.

DAY ❹ MAKING DUMPLINGS

- steaming
- kitchen
- thank
- screamed
- none
- dumplings
- handed
- inside
- tonight

Tonight my mom was steaming some dumplings for supper. She lifted the lid to see if they were finished. "Ouch!" she said and dropped the lid back on. "That's hot. Hyunmin, please hand me a towel."

I handed her a kitchen towel. She carefully lifted the lid and peeked inside.

Then I saw the edge of the towel catch fire. "Oh! Oh!" I yelled.

"Oh! Oh!" my mom screamed and started waving the burning towel in the air.

"Shake it! Don't drop it!" I screamed.

She shook the towel, and the fire went out.

"Thank you, Son," she said.

DAY 5 CHRISTMAS DAY

- smiling
- engagement
- ring
- completely
- whom
- distinguished
- poems
- pointing
- knowingly

I met Sumi for a date tonight. We had dinner and walked by the river. I gave her her Christmas present--a book of poems by some distinguished poet of whom I am completely ignorant. Somehow we ended up wandering through the shops on Jewelry Street.

Sumi stopped suddenly at one counter.

"That's just beautiful!" she said, pointing at a ring with a row of diamonds in it.

"It's an engagement ring," said the saleslady, smiling knowingly at me.

"Oh, really?" Sumi said. Then she took my hand, and we kept walking.

Week 5 /l/, /r/, /n/, /d/

DAY 1 PACKING

- leaving
- later
- cycling
- you're
- room
- fingernails
- New Zealand
- tomorrow
- thirty

I'm taking a three-week cycling trip to New Zealand with Youngjin, and my mom is worried. Tonight, she kept peeking into my room.

"What are you doing?" she said.

"I'm putting music on my MP3 player."

"Shouldn't you be packing? You're leaving for New Zealand tomorrow."

"Yes, Mom. Don't worry about it."

Thirty minutes later, she was back.

"What are you doing?"

"I'm cutting my fingernails."

"Why aren't you packing?"

"I will, Mom. I will."

Thirty minutes later: "Are you packing yet?"

"Please, Mom. I have all night."

DAY 2 LOST AND FOUND

- certainly
- clothes
- lost
- wear
- janitor
- realized
- bench
- thankfully
- assembling

This morning, Youngjin and I landed in Auckland. We found a bench outside the airport and spent two hours assembling our bikes.

Five kilometers from the airport, Youngjin realized he'd left his bag of clothes under the bench.

We rode back and discovered the bag was gone.

"Why don't you check Lost and Found?" I asked.

"I'm scared. I can't speak English," he replied.

"Well, you certainly can't wear the same clothes for three weeks," I said.
I went to Lost and Found for him. Thankfully, a janitor had found the bag and turned it in.

DAY 3 SACRED SOIL

- wall
- memorial
- colonize
- chapter
- sacred
- carved
- native
- soil
- never

Today we visited the Auckland Museum. I spent a long time looking at the war memorial there. Name after name had been carved into the wall. I never knew that there had been war in New Zealand--about thirty years of war to be exact. The fighting was between the native people of New Zealand and the people who had come to colonize the land.

I bought a book of pictures and stories about the New Zealand Wars. It's called *Sacred Soil*. I read the first chapter tonight, and it made me sad.

DAY 4 THE ZOO

• lion	• hurt	• neck
• lounged	• parents	• mud
• slapped	• laughed	• friendly

Youngjin and I decided to go to the zoo today. There was a lion family--a father, mother, and two little cubs. We watched them for almost an hour. The cubs were fighting with each other, but in a friendly way. The two parents lounged in the sun.

Then one cub jumped on its father's neck and bit his ear. The father slapped it on the head with his paw, and the cub fell into the mud.

Youngjin and I laughed until our stomachs hurt.

DAY 5 THE CHOCOLATE FISH CAFÉ

• local	• Lord	• Wellington
• finally	• rings	• only
• chocolate	• arrived	• front

We finally arrived in Wellington today. We only had one day here because tomorrow we catch the bus back to Auckland and our flight to Korea.

We cycled around town for most of the day. Youngjin found something he'd be looking for.

"Look!" he said. "It's the Chocolate Fish Café! Here, take my picture in front of it."

"What for?" I said.

"This café was a local hangout spot for the cast of *The Lord of the Rings.*"

"You're obsessed," I said.

Week 6 /æ/, /ɪ/, /ɛ/, /a/

DAY 1 BADMINTON

- badminton
- after
- racket
- win
- if
- fifth
- herself
- rest
- all

Mina was playing outside today. She was playing badminton all by herself. I asked if I could join her. I wanted to try out a new racket I'd just bought.

After Mina had won the fifth game in a row, I said, "I don't really feel like playing anymore. Let's sit down and rest for a few minutes."

"Oh, please, just one more game? I'll let you win one," she said. That upset me a little.

I like playing badminton with Sumi more. We don't keep score.

DAY 2 A PROTEST

- family
- hands
- song
- imagine
- university
- middle
- protest
- small
- little

I saw a war protest today. The people were marching down the street being led by a van that was blaring the John Lennon song "Imagine."

Most of the marchers were university students. But I saw a small family--mother, father, and child--in the middle of them. The child was young, maybe three years old, and was walking between his parents, holding their hands.

As they passed by me, I saw a sign on the little boy's back. It said, "This baby hates bombs."

DAY ③ ELECTRICITY

• battery	• electricity	• desk
• candles	• fifty	• pretended
• fishing	• clock	• operated

Tonight, I was looking for my battery-operated alarm clock. I was fishing through my desk drawer when I found a box of candles. I don't even know why I have candles in my desk drawer, but I took them out and lit one.

I turned off all the lights in my house and walked around with a candle for the rest of the night. I pretended that I was my grandfather, growing up in the country fifty years ago without electricity.

DAY ④ A NEW JACKET

• jacket	• stylish	• recognize
• actually	• window	• ended
• model	• shopping	• reflection

I went shopping with Sumi today. She wanted to buy a new jacket. She ended up buying a jean jacket with a fur collar. It is warm and actually quite stylish.

Before we left the store, she put her old jacket in the shopping bag and put on the new one. Walking down the street, she saw her reflection in a store window. "Look!" she said. "I don't even recognize myself. I look like a movie star or a model or something."

DAY 5 ANYWHERE

• anxiety	• musician	• anywhere
• practice	• business	• belly
• want	• giving	• pot

Some days I want to be anywhere but here.
Today, Professor Bak told me I should get serious about my guitar playing. "You are a great musician," he said. "You just need to practice more."

My mother told me I needed to work out more. "You're getting a pot belly," she said.

Even Mr. Hong got on my case. "You look bad, man," he said. "You need to get more sleep."

Sometimes I wish everyone would mind their own business. They're only giving me anxiety.

Week·7 /i/, /e/, /o/

DAY ❶ KEYS

• eating	• seeing	• keys
• late	• date	• even
• opened	• borrow	• sofa

Today I was late for work because I couldn't find my house keys. I opened every drawer and closet and cupboard in the house. I looked under the sofa cushions. I even looked to see if I had left them in the front door.

I finally asked my brother Hyunjoon if I could borrow his.

"Sorry," he said. "Tonight's my blind date. We're eating out and then seeing a movie. I don't know what time I'll be home."

I sighed. "Mom!" I cried. "What should I do?"

"Look in your back pocket," she said.

There they were.

DAY ❷ A JUVENILE DELINQUENT

• date	• halfway	• least
• week	• scares	• told
• over	• home	• showed

This morning at breakfast, I asked Hyunjoon about his blind date.

"Well," Hyunjoon said, "I was ready to go home halfway through the date. Over dinner, she told me that she was a juvenile delinquent when she was younger. Now she owns a butcher shop. She wanted to get together again next week. I said no.

Honestly, she scares me."

"Hey, at least she's better than that girl whose boyfriend showed up in the middle of your date," I said.

DAY 3 A WRONG NUMBER

• playing	• oh	• evil
• change	• week	• may
• telephone	• evening	• hello

Hyunjoon's ex-girlfriend still calls our house several times a week. Sometimes I get tired of talking to her. I've threatened to change our phone number.

This evening, I was trying to figure out a new song on my guitar when the telephone rang. I picked it up and said, "Hello. This is Kimbap Heaven. May I help you?"

"Oh! I'm sorry," she said. "I must have the wrong number."

She hung up. I went back to playing my guitar. I am so evil.

DAY 4 THE YEAR OF THE DRAGON

• Chinese	• funny	• say
• favorite	• Saturday	• mate
• supposed to	• slow	• dating

Sumi and I went to our favorite Chinese restaurant for supper on Saturday night. It was our anniversary. We've been dating for three years.

At the restaurant, they had a chart showing the Chinese Lunar Calendar.

"I was born in the year of the dragon," I said. "What

does that say about me?"

"It says that dragons are slow movers, especially when it comes to finding a mate," Sumi said.

"Is that supposed to be funny?" I asked.

DAY 5 CROSSING

• stream	• row	• old
• today	• shallow	• growing
• people	• elbow	• afraid

Today I took a walk by the stream near my house. There is a row of rocks across the stream so that people can cross it. I saw an old man trying to step on the first rock, but his foot slipped and fell into the shallow water.

No one stopped to help him, so I grabbed his elbow, and we crossed the stream together. Then he went his way, and I went mine.

Sometimes I'm afraid of growing old.

You Too Can Speak English
Pronunciation Guide

LEVEL 6

Week·1 /s/, /z/, /š/

DAY 1 SHOES

- seriously
- what's
- dumbest
- recognize
- size
- sometimes
- shoes
- God's
- yours

Hyunjoon and I each own a pair of the same shoes. They are even the same size. Sometimes it's hard to recognize which shoes are his and which are mine.

Today, as Hyunjoon and I were leaving the house, I stopped and stared at my shoes.

"What's wrong?" Hyunjoon asked.

"I think one of these shoes might be yours and the other one is mine," I said.

We both looked seriously at the shoes for a long time.

Then Hyunjoon said, "We must be the dumbest people on God's green earth. Let's go."

DAY 2 NOSTALGIA

- understand
- nostalgia
- listened
- mesmerizing
- several
- songs
- Spanish
- she
- instruments

Today I saw a Bolivian band named Nostalgia playing in a courtyard downtown. I sat on a bench and listened to several songs. They played some instruments I'd never seen before. All of the songs were in Spanish, so I couldn't understand what they were saying, but the music was mesmerizing. I tapped my feet to the rhythm.

I saw a lady on another bench, and she was singing along with all of their songs. She must be a big fan.

DAY 3 POPSICLES

• Popsicle	• strawberry	• sunshine
• drops	• stood	• shirt
• surprisingly	• shop	• appreciating

Today was a surprisingly warm winter day. To celebrate, I ate a strawberry Popsicle after lunch. I stood outside the snack shop and ate it, appreciating the sunshine. I smiled at everyone who passed by.
"It's a beautiful day, isn't it?" I said to anyone who smiled back. When I was finished eating, I walked to class.

"What's on your shirt?" Professor Bak asked when I walked in.

I looked down and saw little pink drops of strawberry Popsicle. **sigh**

DAY 4 A SECRET

• secret	• sweet	• shades
• asleep	• sure	• fish
• stuffed	• said	• psychiatrist

"Can I tell you a secret?" Youngjin asked me today.

"Sure," I said.

"Don't laugh at me," he said.

"I won't," I replied.

"I still sleep with a stuffed animal. I can't fall asleep without it. I've had it since I was a kid."

"What is it?" I asked.

"It's a big yellow fish. The yellow has faded by several shades, but I still love it."

"That's really...sweet," I said, "but maybe you should see a psychiatrist."

DAY 5 PUNISHMENT

• stubborn	• freeze	• sister
• guess	• apologized	• outside
• congratulations	• kids	• surprised

"Guess what!" Mr. Hong said to me today.

"What?" I replied.

"We're going to have another baby!"

"Congratulations," I said. "Are you ready for two kids?"

"I don't know," he said. "I'm worried about them fighting. My sister and I fought all the time when we were kids. My parents would make us sit outside on the front step until we apologized, even in the winter. We were so stubborn, I'm surprised we didn't freeze to death."

Week · 2 /č/, /ǰ/, /z/

DAY 1 MUD

• adventure	• beaches	• dozens
• joke	• seagulls	• chased
• suggested	• journey	• revenge

Youngjin and I needed an adventure. Youngjin suggested taking a journey to the Yellow Sea, so we hopped in his car and hit the road. The beaches we went to were not sandy or rocky. They were mud flats.

Dozens of seagulls sat on the shore. We chased them. We threw big rocks in the mud and listened to them splat. Youngjin made some kind of a joke, so I playfully pushed him. He lost his balance and fell down in the mud. Oops! He got his revenge by smearing mud on my face.

It was a good day.

DAY 2 IRONING

• much	• watch	• gives
• marriage	• clothes	• days
• husband	• knows	• does

Every day I watch my mom iron my dad's shirts and pants. I don't ever see him thank her for it.

Today I asked her a question.

"Why do you iron Dad's clothes every day? What does he ever do for you?"

"It's how he knows I love him," my mom said. "And,

you know, marriage isn't always 50/50 give and take. Some days, one person gives more. Some days, the other one does. You won't always receive as much as you give. Learn that now, and you'll make a much better husband someday."

DAY ③ CHICKEN

- chicken
- natural
- gently
- chirped
- just
- mouths
- vegetarian
- was
- his

I had a dream last night about chickens. Everyone in my dream was walking around with baby chickens in their mouths. They weren't eating them or anything. They were just gently carrying them around.

I saw Hyunjoon in my dream. I said hello. A little chick poked its head out of his mouth and chirped at me.

I found a chick and put it in my mouth too. It seemed like the natural thing to do.

But then Hyunjoon and the people around me started to die.

Maybe I should become a vegetarian.

DAY ④ DANGER

- picture
- danger
- large
- always
- teacher
- is
- generally
- days
- questions

My English teacher, Kate, is trying to learn Korean. She generally asks me questions every few days. Today I asked her what her favorite Korean word is.

"*We-hum*--danger," she said. "I always picture a group of people walking down the street humming. They are completely unaware that a large piano is about to fall out of the sky and land on them--like in a cartoon. Get it? We hum? Danger?"

I didn't get it. Something was lost in translation.

DAY 5 MY SENSES

- furniture
- sewage
- music
- concerto
- each
- breeze
- cello
- individual
- exercising

Today I tried exercising my senses. I paid careful attention to each individual sound and smell around me.

When I passed a furniture shop, I smelled the wood and the finish on the furniture. When I passed a music institute, I heard someone make a mistake while playing a concerto on the cello. A breeze blew by, and I caught the scent of goldenbells, and I knew that spring was on its way.

I tried to ignore the sewage drain as I passed by.

Week·3 /r/, /w/, /kw/

DAY 1 THE NEWS

• world	• current	• terrorist
• worried	• aware	• freak
• earthquake	• watching	• reputation

I try to be aware of current events, but I have a hard time watching the news without getting worried.

Hyunjoon and I watched a segment tonight about a terrorist attack in the West Bank. Then there was a segment about a freak ice storm in Los Angeles and an earthquake in southern Italy. There have been so many disasters lately.

"Do you think the world is coming to an end?" Hyunjoon asked me. He has a reputation for asking really hard questions.

"Maybe," I said quietly.

DAY 2 BUS DRIVERS

• driver	• whenever	• quality
• wonderful	• waved	• direction
• riding	• work	• 1451

Today I was riding the bus home from work--Bus 1451. When I first got on the bus, the driver smiled at me and said hello. Then, as we passed another Bus 1451 going the other direction, he waved enthusiastically at the other driver.

Wow! He's quality, I thought. I get a wonderful feeling whenever I see a person who really has fun with their job. I hope that I can always do my job with the same kind of joy.

DAY 3 THE PAPER SHREDDER

• ruler	• safer	• turn
• quickly	• shredder	• work
• grab	• fingers	• figure

Today at work I dropped a pen, and it landed in the paper shredder. It landed right against the blades. I stared at it for a long time, trying to figure out how to get it out.

First, I quickly poked at it with my fingers, but I was too scared to really grab ahold of it. I didn't want to shred my fingers.

Then I got a ruler and slid it around until the pen popped out. The safer thing to do would have been to turn the shredder off, but I didn't think of that.

DAY 4 IN THE MIRROR

• across	• reflection	• hurried
• doorway	• mirror	• consequently
• reason	• walking	• weird

Something weird happened to me today. I was walking by a doorway, and for some reason I thought it was a mirror. A shadow moved across it, and I thought it was my reflection. I stopped to look at myself, but instead, I saw a man walking out of the door toward me.

"Yikes!" I yelled.

"Yikes!" he yelled back.

"Sorry," I said, and hurried on.

Consequently, I was afraid to look in the mirror for the rest of the day.

DAY 5 SPRING

• flower	• princess	• spring
• swinging	• throwing	• quietly
• park	• world	• brushed

It is spring. Sumi and I walked around a small park near my home this evening. The park is on the top of a hill. As we came down the hill, we were swinging our hands. Blossoms were quietly falling around us. The stairs were covered in flower petals.

"Oh!" Sumi said, "I feel like a princess. The entire world is throwing flowers at my feet. Don't you love the spring?"

I smiled and gently brushed a petal from her hair.

Week 4 endings -/č/, /ǰ/, -ed, -s

DAY 1 MY ADDICTION

- sandwich
- started
- McDonald's
- McMuffins
- addicted
- charge
- concerned
- much
- porridge

I've gotten into the habit of sleeping in and then running to class at the last minute. My mother is getting concerned.

"Please eat something," she says. "Have some rice or porridge or something."

"I'll be okay, Mom," I say as I charge out the door.

She doesn't know that I've started getting breakfast at McDonald's on the way to school. I love Egg McMuffins so much. They are the perfect sandwich. I am addicted. I can't stop eating them.

DAY 2 SNACKS

- yelled
- covered
- opened
- whispered
- nodded
- poured
- lights
- diamonds
- peanuts

Tonight Sumi and I were watching the city lights from the hilltop park. She was a little sad because her boss had yelled at her today.

"I brought your favorite snack," I said. "Chocolate-covered peanuts. Do you want some?"

"Sure," she said.

I opened the bag and poured some into her hand. There, in the middle of the peanuts, lay a ring with a row of diamonds in it. She stared at it. Her eyes lit up.

"What do you think, Sumi?" I said. "Will you marry me?"

She nodded. "Yes," she whispered.

DAY 3 FINGERNAILS

• smudge	• painted	• fingernails
• strange	• looked	• hearts
• touch	• asked	• hands

I saw Mina playing outside our building today. She was waving her hands in the air. It looked kind of strange.

"What are you doing?" I asked her.

"Drying my fingernails," she said. "My dad painted them for me. I'll show them to you, but you can't touch them. They're still wet."

I looked closely. Her nails were pink with little red hearts on them. They had been painted very carefully. Not a smudge or a bump.

"Your dad is quite the manicurist," I said.

DAY 4 A SINGING TREE

• emerge	• stared	• branches
• scratched	• noticed	• minutes
• catch	• seemed	• paused

I was walking by a tree outside the music building today. As I passed, I noticed that the tree seemed to be singing.

Wow! That tree must be full of birds, I thought.

I stepped closer and stared up into the branches, trying to catch a glimpse of the mysterious, melodious birds. Nothing. People paused as they were walking by and looked up at the tree to see what I was staring at. Still nothing. I stood there for three full minutes and never saw a single bird emerge. Finally, I just scratched my head and walked away.

DAY 5 STALKING HYUNJOON

• couch	• urge	• punched
• kids	• heritage	• approached
• adopted	• accomplished	• landed

Hyunjoon was sitting on the couch watching TV today. He was watching a show about kids being adopted from Korea and how they reconnect with their Korean heritage. He was really into the program. I had the sudden urge to attack him.

I slowly approached him from behind. Then... "ROAR!" I yelled as I jumped over the couch and landed on top of him.

"What in the world?" he yelled. "You're crazy!" He punched me on the shoulder.

Mission accomplished.

Week · 5 /ə/, /U/, /u/, /yu/

DAY 1 SPELL CHECK

• hymnbook
• afternoon
• other
• brother
• done
• must
• occurred
• humiliating
• you

I wrote an email to Kate today. I did a quick spell check before I mailed it. It kept saying that I had spelled Hyunjoon's name wrong. I clicked *Ignore* and kept going. There weren't any other mistakes. I was very pleased with myself.

She wrote back later this afternoon. "Why do you call your brother Hymnbook?" she asked me. "For a nickname, that's outright strange."

Then it occurred to me what I'd done. Instead of clicking on *Ignore*, I had clicked on *Correct*.

The spell checker had decided my brother's name must be Hymnbook.
How humiliating!

DAY 2 UNIFORMS

• police
• school
• shoes
• looking
• younger
• suit
• cool
• uniform
• put

Today I was looking at a brochure for a police academy. It reminded me that when I was younger, I always thought it would be cool to have a job where I could wear a uniform. Police officer. Firefighter. Baseball player.

Then I went to middle school and had to wear a

uniform every day. It wasn't that exciting anymore.
Thankfully, as a guitarist, I can always change my look. Sometimes I can wear jeans and no shoes. Other times I can put on a suit.

DAY 3 ELVIS

• love	• shook	• movies
• would	• student	• humorous
• continued	• front	• used to

In class today, Professor Bak started talking about Elvis.

"You know," he said, "I used to love watching Elvis movies. I was a big fan. I would even stand in front of the mirror and try to dance like Elvis."

He shook his hips for us. "As you can see, I never really got the hang of it."

Then he continued his lecture.

"That's just weird," I whispered to the student next to me.

"I think it's rather humorous," he replied.

DAY 4 WRAPPING PAPER

• today	• cookbook	• classroom
• use	• food	• what
• because	• from	• away

We had a going-away party for Kate today. She is leaving Korea next week. Our class bought her a nice set of chopsticks and placemats. We got her a Korean cookbook too because she loves Korean food.

I helped her clean up the classroom after the party. She held up the wrapping paper from her gifts.

"This is handmade Korean paper. I don't want to throw it away," she said. "What do you think, Hyunmin? What can I use this for?"

"I don't know," I said.

DAY 5 BORN INTO BROTHELS

• whatever	• cameras	• documentary
• support	• looked	• prostitution
• India	• rescued	• photography

Tonight I watched a documentary called *Born into Brothels.* It is about a lady who taught photography to children growing up in the brothels of Calcutta, India. The kids looked so happy as they carried their cameras around the city, snapping pictures of whatever they saw. Now the lady sells their pictures to support their education. She has rescued them from a life of prostitution and poverty.

I would like to change someone's world like that. I need a vision.

Week·6 /ay/, /aw/, /oy/

DAY ❶ LIGHTNING

- avoid
- lightning
- strikes
- highest
- points
- crouch
- ground
- tried
- how

There was a thunderstorm today. As I dashed from class to the bus, I tried to remember how to avoid being struck by lightning. The only thing I could remember was that lightning strikes usually occur on the head or shoulders. That's because they are the highest points on the human body. It's always a good idea to crouch close to the ground if you're stranded in a thunderstorm.

I tried to think of more thunderstorm safety hints, but that's all I could remember.

I used to know these things.

DAY ❷ SWITCHED AT BIRTH

- fight
- outsider
- enjoyment
- tonight
- sometimes
- point
- smiling
- joins
- about

No one else in my family really joins in my enjoyment of music. I tried playing a song on the guitar for my mom and brother tonight. They listened at first, but then they started talking. By the end, they were having a fight about whether or not Hyunjoon had taken out the trash.

"That's it," I said, smiling hopefully. "That's the end of my song."

"That was beautiful," my mother said, pretending to have listened.

What's the point of trying? I wonder if maybe I was switched at birth. Sometimes I feel like an outsider in my own home.

DAY 3 SUMI'S BIRTHDAY

- items
- outfit
- employees
- silent
- powder
- foundation
- eyebrows
- counters
- nice

Today I went shopping for a nice gift to give to Sumi. Her birthday is coming up. I walked through the department store and saw counters full of powder and foundation and facial scrubs. The store employees either raised their eyebrows at me or gave me the silent treatment. I have no knowledge of health and beauty items. I think I'll leave that to her girlfriends.

I saw a nice outfit hanging on the rack, but then I remembered what she said about my taste in clothes. Maybe I'll just give her another book.

DAY 4 A THOUSAND POUNDS

- idea
- thousand
- pounds
- boy
- noise
- loudly
- driving
- like
- minor

Today, Youngjin was staring intently at a piece of paper and chewing loudly on his pen.

"Dude!" I said. "Stop chewing on your pen. That noise is driving me crazy!"

"Sorry," he said. "I can't figure this out. How many pounds are in a kilogram?"

"2.2," I said.

"Boy, I was way off," he said. "I thought I weighed like a thousand pounds."

"Let me see that," I said.

He handed me his paper. Sure enough, he had written: 1 kilogram = 22 pounds.

"I had an idea that I was forgetting something," he said. "It's such a minor detail."

DAY 5 ALUMINUM FOIL

• justify	• proud	• now
• foil	• out	• mouth
• deny	• trying	• I'm

I went to the dentist today. It was just a regular checkup. I've only had one cavity in my life, and I'm very proud of that.

Out of curiosity, I asked my dentist a question. "Is it really true that if you chew on aluminum foil when you have a filling, it will hurt like mad?"

"If you had a silver filling, it would," she said. "But yours is porcelain. Now, I would not use that as an excuse to justify your sticking tin foil in your mouth."

"I can't deny that I thought about trying it," I said.

Week·7 vowels plus /r/

DAY ❶ PERSONAL SPACE

• personal	• arm's	• comfortable
• Ireland	• backward	• here
• worry	• different	• there's

Today I asked Kate how life in Ireland is different from life in Korea.

"People in Ireland need lots of personal space," she said. "They don't like people to stand too close to them when they talk. They feel most comfortable when there's at least an arm's length between them."

I took a big step backward.

She laughed. "Don't worry. I've gotten used to less personal space here in Korea. I will miss the coziness of riding the subway at 8:00 a.m."

DAY ❷ TOUCH

• elderly	• number	• years
• delivering	• warming	• worked
• arm	• supper	• considered

Today, I worked with the Red Cross delivering lunches to elderly people. One old woman cried when I gave her a lunch. I put my arm around her.

"No one has touched me in a long time," she said. "Thank you."

I'd never considered how much I touch my own mother. I thought about it and could count on one hand the number of times I've hugged her in twenty-five years.

When I got home, I saw my mother was warming some *chigae* for supper. I threw my arms around her.

"What's wrong with you?" she said.

"Nothing," I replied.

DAY 3 AIRPLANES

• dark	• remember	• returning
• airplane	• somewhere	• Norway
• more	• over	• Turkey

Today, Kate left for Ireland. When we said good-bye, she told me, "I will always pray for you. Remember that."

Tonight I looked out my window and watched an airplane fly across the dark sky and disappear. I thought of Kate up in the air, somewhere over Turkey or maybe Norway, eating pretzels and returning to her home and family.

I learned more than just English in Kate's class. She taught me many things--about peace and hope and faith. I will miss her.

DAY 4 BUTTER

• butter	• lover	• before
• organic	• turned	• regular
• grocery	• never	• argued

My mom sent me to the grocery store for butter this afternoon. I couldn't find the butter that we usually buy. I had a few extra thousand won, so I decided to try some organic butter. We've never tried it before.

When I brought it home, my mom and I argued about the extra money I'd spent. But then I mixed some of the butter with rice and a little bit of soy sauce and had her try a bite.

"That really *does* taste better than regular butter," she said. "I think you've turned me into an organic butter lover!"

DAY 5 THE FUTURE

• guitar	• mysterious	• support
• wherever	• circus	• future
• prepared	• advertising	• normal

I saw a sign today advertising the circus. I had a random thought. *Someday, when I have kids, I want to take them to the circus.*

That led to more thoughts about kids, marriage and the future.

My future is mysterious to me. Sometimes it worries me. Is that normal? I do know that wherever I go, Sumi will be with me. I'll have my guitar to play. I'll have the support of a family that loves me. Beyond that, I don't know what life has prepared for me, but I think am ready for it.

God, go with me.

CHARTS & PICTURES

Foreword

This book is an essential companion to the series, *You Too Can Speak English* as it contains the nineteen charts and five pictures used in many of the exercises throughout the series. Since the pictures are somewhat limited in scope and their use is explained in the lessons themselves, suggestions here will be restricted to the charts.

The purpose of charts in the SDA English program is to establish almost immediate fluency in new grammatical constructions by means of a series of sentences containing familiar vocabulary. On the basis of this initial fluency, the new grammar point is then extended into wider vocabulary ranges and communication situations with exercises not based on the charts.

Introducing the charts

Each chart has a number of basic sentences. It is important that students memorize these basic sentences when the chart is introduced. For the connected exercises to be effective, time should be spent on practicing the correct pronunciation of the vocabulary. All of the charts can be conveniently introduced in the following way: the teacher says the first basic sentence several times at natural conversation speed, and students repeat in chorus. After choral repetition, individual students are called on to say the sentence, until good re-production is achieved. The same procedure is used for the other pictures. The teacher can then call for choral or individual reproduction of the sentences in random order. At this point (not before) students can be asked to read the basic sentence while repeating the sentences after the teacher one last time.

Once a chart has been well learned in this way, students are free to concentrate on meaning, stress, intonation and rhythm when using the chart in later lessons for more complex sentence structures.

Choral use of charts

In many cases, chart exercises can be done chorally, since the contents of a chart are completely familiar to the students. This is valuable because a part of each class period is thereby given to active speaking practice by all students, even in large groups.

For choral work to be effective, the students should be trained to speak in unison in order to attain natural English rhythm and stress from the beginning. Chart exercises are ideally suited for this training as it is possible to maintain the same sentence-intonation and rhythm throughout a complete drill. The teacher can guide the rhythm with hand movements or by tapping the desk while presenting the initial examples. A group of twenty or thirty students can be taught to produce even long and complex sentences in unison with natural intonation using this method. This is rewarding for the teacher and sets the stage for communication practice and freer conversation in each lesson.

Scope of the charts

These examples of possible exercises with charts illustrate how useful they are in the classroom.

Chart 11 presents verbs of motion and associated prepositions. There are twelve picture frames and 12 basic sentences. The first three actions are:

1. Luke is swimming across the lake.
2. Shawn is getting out of the car.
3. Tom is climbing up the tree.

Here then are some exercises, cued and uncued, based on this chart.

● Example 1

Verb phrase + -ING pattern. Single cues.

1.	Teacher	have a lot of trouble
	S.1	Luke had a lot of trouble swimming across the lake.
2.	Teacher	bump his head
	S.2	Shawn bumped his head getting out of the car.
3.	Teacher	hurt his arm
	S.3	Tom hurt his arm climbing up the tree.

● Example 2

To contrast various verb patterns. Q&A with double cues.

1.	Teacher	the swimming coach - watch
	S.1	What did the swimming coach watch Luke do?
	S.2	He watched him swim across the lake.
2.	Teacher	the driver - make
	S.3	What did the driver make Shawn do?
	S.4	He made him get out of the car.
3.	Teacher	Tom's friends - challenge
	S.5	What did Tom's friends challenge him to do?
	S.6	They challenged him to climb up the tree.

● Example 3
Uncued conversation exercise.

1. S.1 Look! There's a boy swimming across the lake.
   S.2 I wonder who it is.
   S.1 Maybe it's Luke.

2. S.3 Look! There's a man getting out of the car.
   S.4 I wonder who it is.
   S.3 Maybe it's Shawn.

3. S.5 Look! There's a boy climbing up the tree.
   S.6 I wonder who it is.
   S.5 Maybe it's Tom.

● Example 4
Uncued conversation exercise.

1. S.1 I'm looking for Luke. Do you know where he is?
   S.2 Can't you see him over there?
   He's swimming across the lake.
2. S.3 I'm looking for Shawn. Do you know where he is?
   S.4 Can't you see him over there?
   He's getting out of the car.
3. S.5 I'm looking for Tom. Do you know where he is?
   S.6 Can't you see him over there?
   He's climbing up the tree.

이 도표는 *You Too Can Speak English*의 연습을 위하여 여러 번에 걸쳐 사용되고 있습니다, 목적은, 영어의 문형(文型)을 자동적으로 익히는 데 도움이 되게 하는 것입니다. 도표가 교과서에 도입되면, 교사가 도표와 그림의 사용법을 설명하기 때문에 도표에 나타난 그림의 대상, 동작에 즉시 익숙해져서 새로운 단어에 주의를 집중시키지 않을지라도 문형의 연습이 차츰 이루어지게 되어 있습니다. 도표를 근거로 한 연습은 먼저 교사가 한 두 개의 그림을 사용하여 예를 들어주기 때문에 계속해서 나머지 그림을 사용해서 연습하십시오,

될 수 있는 대로 빨리 이야기하게끔 교사를 따라 반복하는 기회를 놓치지 않도록 노력하십시오. 그렇게 하면 영어의 기본문형을 의식하지 않고 자유롭게 사용할 수 있게 됩니다. 일상생활에 즉시 도움이 될 것이므로 끊임없이 이용해 주십시오.

You Too Can
Speak English

CHART I

HIGH
LOW
Nicole Gibson
1

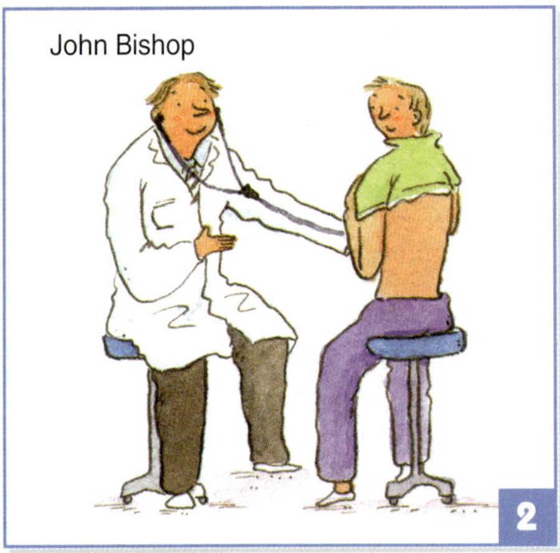
John Bishop
2

Joe Richards
3

Sarah Jones
4

Bob Smith
5

George Brown
6

Mary McBride
7

Lance King
8

Dave Jordan
9

Jenny Clark
10

Susan Green
11

James Walton
12

CHART 2

7

8

9

CHART 3

7

8

9

10

11

12

CHART 4

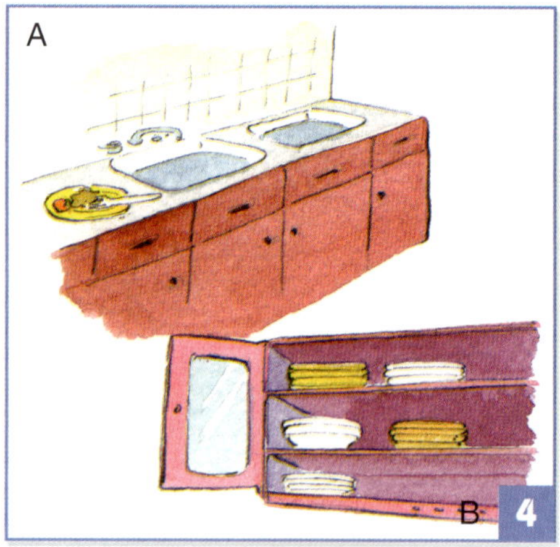

A
B
7

A
B
8

A
B
9

CHART 5

A
Bob
Tom
B
1

A
Bill
Ken
B
2

A
Scott
Mr. Jones
B
3

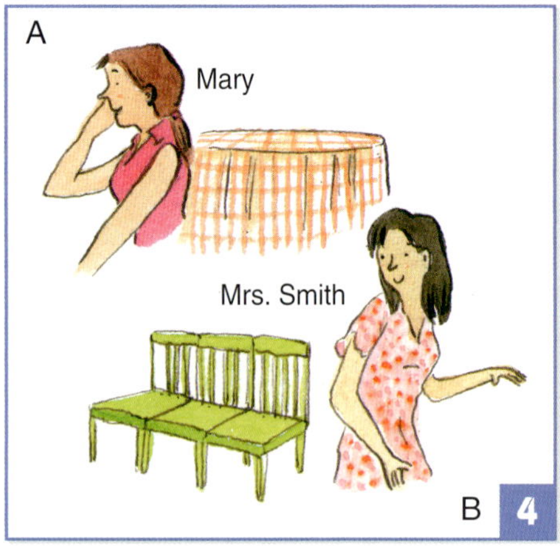
A
Mary
Mrs. Smith
B
4

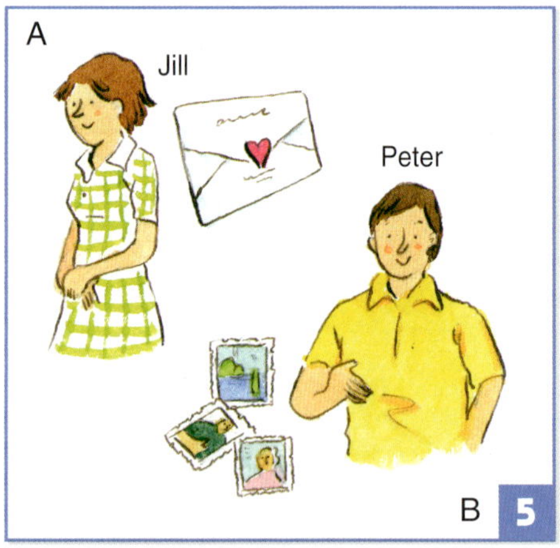
A
Jill
Peter
B
5

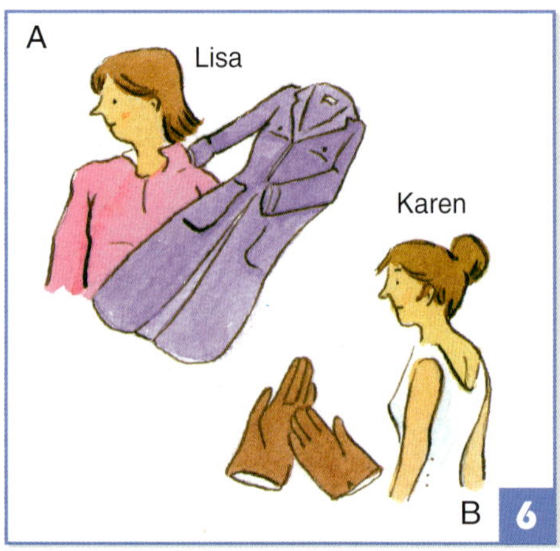
A
Lisa
Karen
B
6

A
Mrs. Ramsey
Mr. Olsen
B
7

A
Emily
Ann
B
8

A
Mrs. Reid
Mrs. Lee
B
9

CHART 6

A
Ron
Steve
BUS
Lisa
B
1

A
Janet
Mr. Johnson
and his family
B
2

A
John
Ann
Jim
B
3

A
Mr. and Mrs.
Woodhouse
George
B
4

A
Bill
Ken
SUB WAY
Chris
B
5

A
Mrs. Andrews
Mary
Mr. Andrews
B
6

A
Paul
Ryan
Larry
B
7

A
Kyle
CAMPING SITE
Bob
Mr. Oh
B
8

A
Mr. Miller
Mrs. Miller
and her friend
B
9

CHART 7

A
Why can't people keep appointments?
Can I make my appointment for a later day?
Mrs. Humphrey
B
1

A
Now I feel better!
Mr. Rivers
No, thanks. I don't want any.
B
2

A
Thank you.
Mrs. Harrison
It's very poor quality.
B
3

A
Maybe it's too long.
Mrs. Jones
FITTING ROOM
I hope it fits me.
B
4

A
I'm glad that's finished.
Mr. Black
At last!
B
5

A
That's it! I'm finished.
Charles
This is very difficult.
B
6

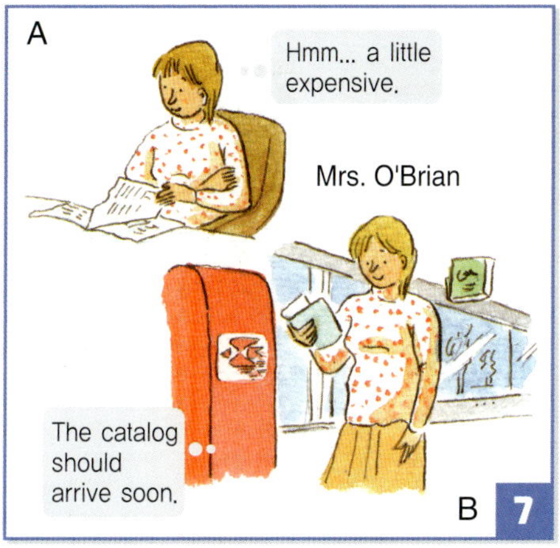
A
Hmm... a little expensive.
Mrs. O'Brian
The catalog should arrive soon.
B
7

A
Everything is correct now.
Susan
I need to type this again.
B
8

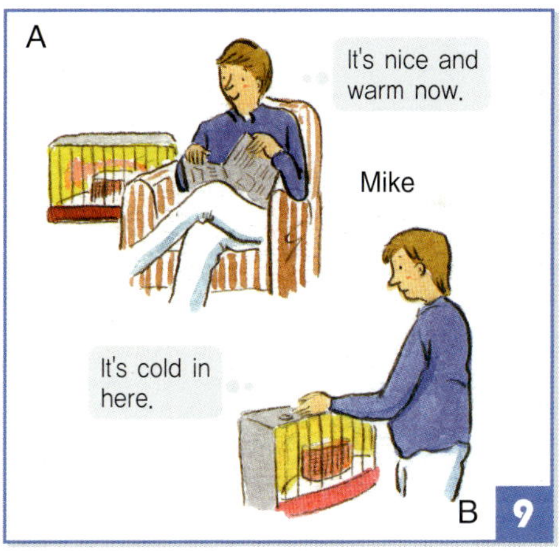
A
It's nice and warm now.
Mike
It's cold in here.
B
9

CHART 8

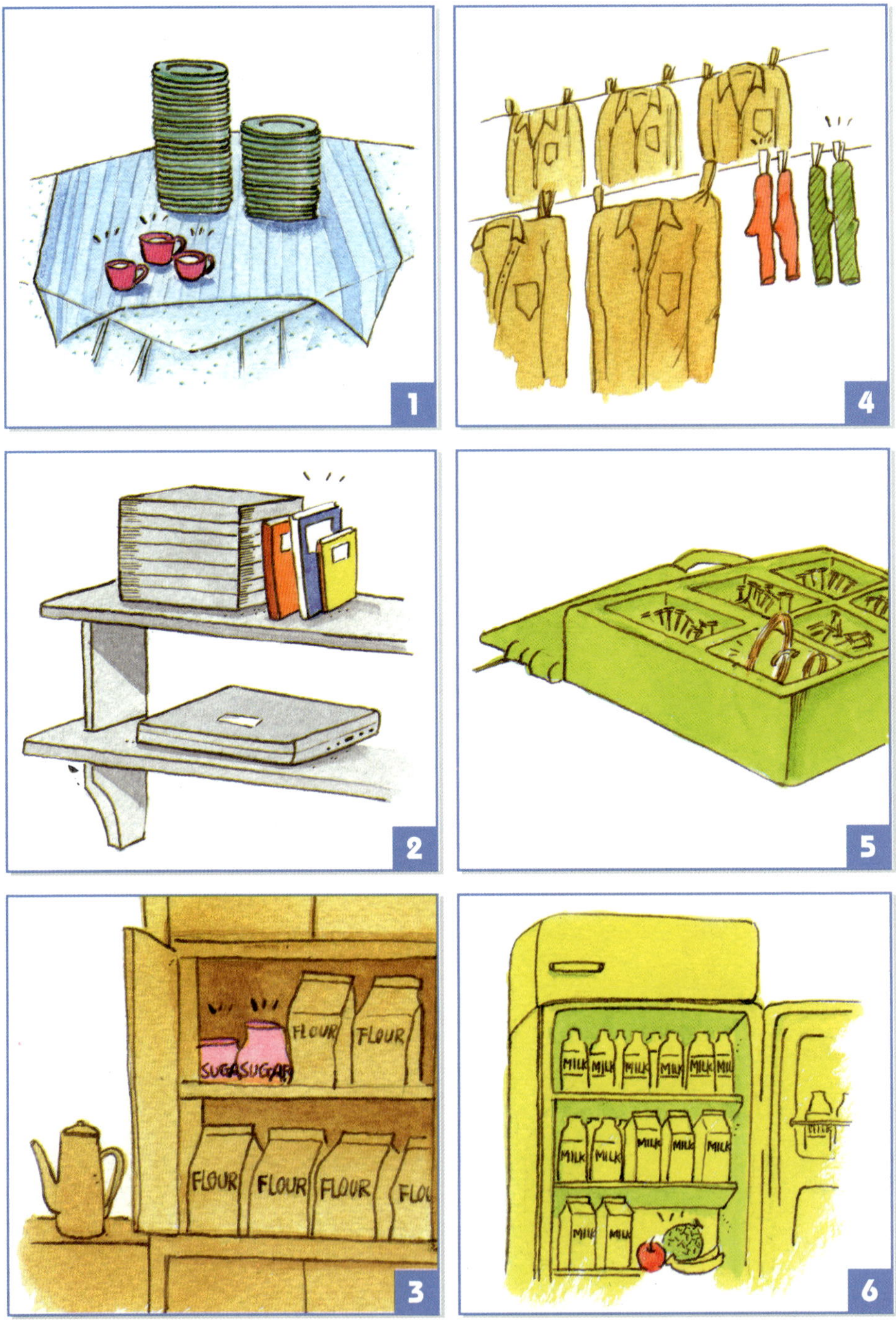

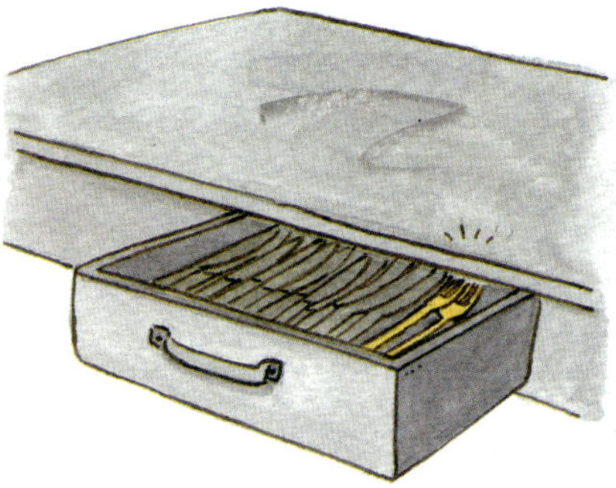
7

8

9

10

11

12

CHART 9

Thank you, young man.
Simon
1

Mr. Conroy
Have you heard the one about...?
2

They're almost ready. Call the boys.
Mrs. Rivers
3

How much is that?
Philip
4

$50
Mrs. Hall
Can you give me a receipt, please?
5

Adam
"Hi, Charlie, wish you were here..."
6

Dad gets a lot of letters.
Scott
7

Professor Grant
This is a good firm, and they pay well.
10

Mr. Collins
Thank you, sir.
8

Mr. Reagan
You can get 20 miles to the gallon.
11

They're very nice, Timmy.
Timmy
9

Mrs. Black
I hope it's still hot.
12

CHART 10

John
Peter
J
6

John
Peter
7

John
Peter
8

CHART II

1

4

2

5

3

6

Olsen
7

The mailman
10

Katie
8

Heather
11

The Gregsons
9

Timmy
12

CHART 12

Jake
7

Mrs. Gregson
10

8

11

9

12

CHART 13

7

8

4:00
6:00
9

6:45
10

7:00
11

12

CHART 14

1

2

3

4

5

6

7

8

9

BANK
10

11

12

CHART 15

1

2

3

4

5

6

7

8

9

CHART 16

1

2

3

4

5

6

7

8

9

10

11

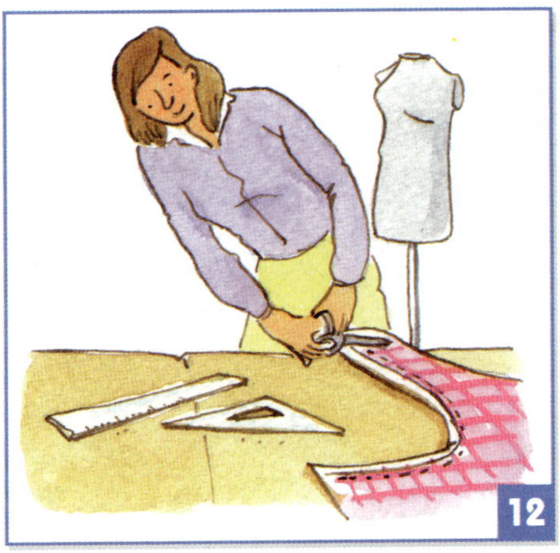

12

CHART 17

Amy Wheeler
PATENT SECTION
1

NEW PLANS
Mark Scotti
CONFI-DENTIAL
2

Karen Hyde
3

NEW PRODUCTS
David Levitzky
4

Susan Brady
ADVERTISING SECTION
5

Kevin Bloom
OUR COMPANY
6

Ben Keenan
7

Mary Peterson
PRESIDENT
8

ON STRIKE
Jack Martin
9

CHART 18

1

2

3

4

5

6

7

8

9

10

11

12

CHART 19

A

The new office should help sales in that area.

B **1**

A

I need last month's statistics too.

B **2**

A

It would help to know their language.

B **3**

A

Enough! I have other things to do.

B **4**

A

They're moving up –
we need something new.

B **5**

A

These products
look good.

B **6**

A
The whole section is inefficient.
We have to do something.
EXECUTIVE DIRECTOR
B
7

A
What's the dollar equivalent of these prices?
FINANCIAL OFFICER
Dollar/Yen EXCHANGE RATES
B
8

A
Bring Tom in here. I have some ideas.
MANAGING DIRECTOR
IDEA FILE
B
9

PICTURE I

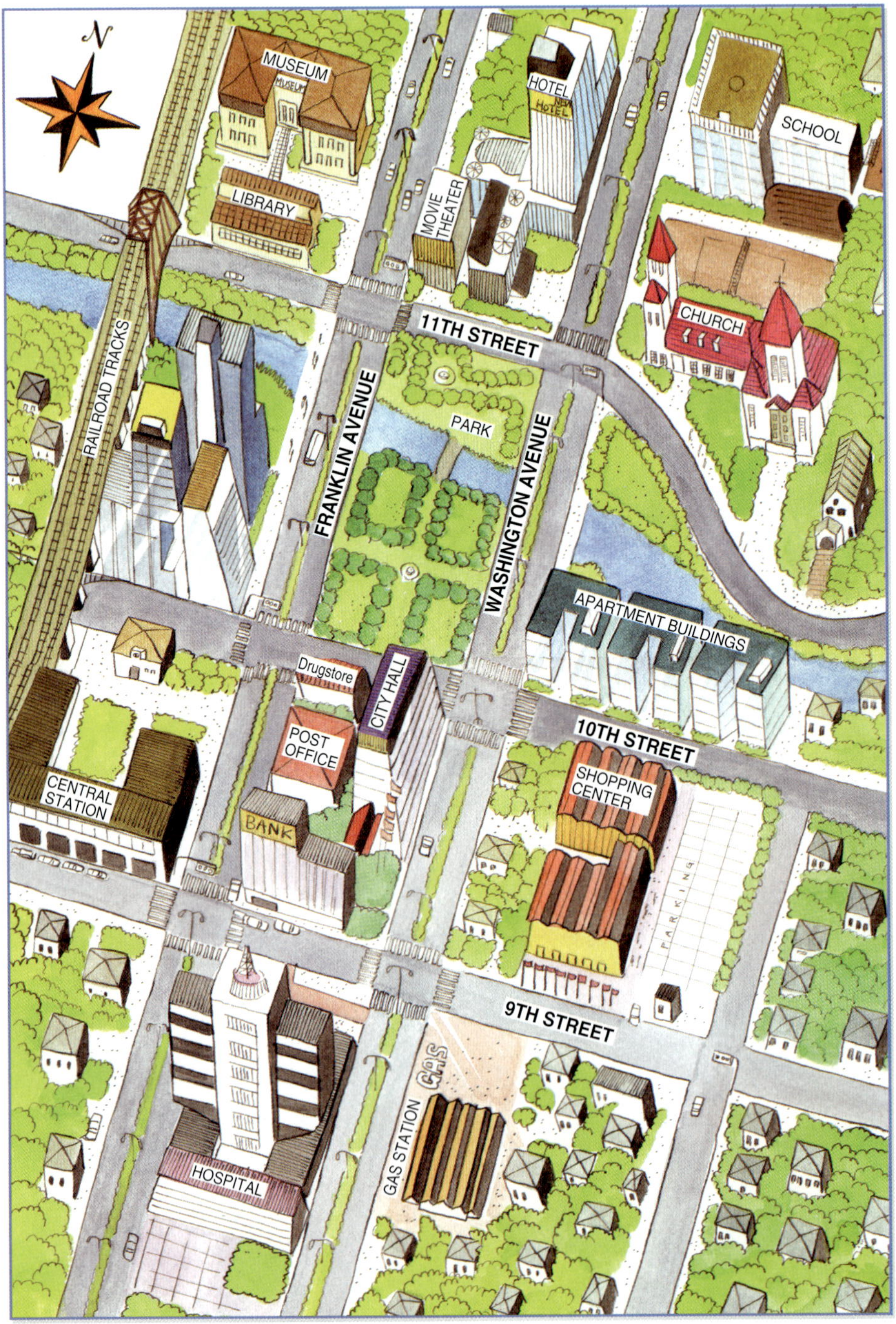
N
MUSEUM
MUSEUM
LIBRARY
HOTEL
NEW HOTEL
SCHOOL
MOVIE THEATER
CHURCH
11TH STREET
RAILROAD TRACKS
PARK
FRANKLIN AVENUE
WASHINGTON AVENUE
APARTMENT BUILDINGS
Drugstore
CITY HALL
POST OFFICE
10TH STREET
SHOPPING CENTER
CENTRAL STATION
BANK
PARKING
9TH STREET
GAS
GAS STATION
HOSPITAL

PICTURE 2

PICTURE 3

PICTURE 4

4
5
6
7
8
9
10
11
12
13
14

PICTURE 5

(B)
(D)
11
12
13
14
15
16
17
18
19
20
33
34
35
36
37
38
39
40
41
42
43
44
45

1. Various occupations

1. Nicole Gibson is a teacher.
2. John Bishop is a doctor.
3. Joe Richards is an engineer.
4. Sarah Jones is a homemaker.
5. Bob Smith is a photographer.
6. George Brown is a professional golfer.
7. Mary McBride is a nurse.
8. Lance King is a reporter.
9. Dave Jordan is a mechanic.
10. Jenny Clark is a flight attendant.
11. Susan Green is a graphic designer.
12. James Walton is a salesman.

2. Corresponding activities

1. Nicole Gibson is a teacher. She teaches English.
2. John Bishop is a doctor. He examines patients.
3. Joe Richards is an engineer. He designs machines.
4. Sarah Jones is a homemaker. She looks after her family.
5. Bob Smith is a photographer. He takes photographs.
6. George Brown is a professional golfer. He plays in tournaments.
7. Mary McBride is a nurse. She takes care of patients.
8. Lance King is a reporter. He writes articles.
9. Dave Jordan is a mechanic. He repairs cars.
10. Jenny Clark is a flight attendant. She serves passengers.
11. Susan Green is a graphic designer. She creates layouts.
12. James Walton is a salesman. He sells appliances.

CHART • 2

basic sentences

1. Singular and plural nouns: containers and things they contain

1. This is a bookcase. These are books.
2. This is a cupboard. These are dishes.
3. This is a closet. These are clothes.
4. This is a drawer. These are shirts.
5. This is a refrigerator. These are vegetables.
6. This is a locker. These are work clothes.
7. This is a shelf. These are CDs.
8. This is a toolbox. These are tools.
9. This is a safe. These are valuables.

2. With the verb *KEEP*

1. He keeps his books in the bookcase.
2. She keeps her dishes in the cupboard.
3. They keep their clothes in the closet.
4. He keeps his shirts in the drawer.
5. She keeps her vegetables in the refrigerator.
6. He keeps his work clothes in the locker.
7. They keep their CDs on the shelf.
8. He keeps his tools in the toolbox.
9. They keep their valuables in the safe.

CHART • 3

Verb phrases used to introduce the past tense

1. He listened to English tapes this morning.
2. They played cards yesterday.
3. She practiced the piano last Sunday.
4. He memorized the dialogue yesterday evening.
5. He visited his relatives last week.
6. She washed the dishes this afternoon.
7. They watched TV last night.
8. He worked yesterday afternoon.
9. She typed the report a few hours ago.
10. They got together with their friends last night.
11. She ironed the clothes last Monday.
12. They attended the seminar last month.

CHART • 4 basic sentences

Expressions of place and position

1. The glass on the table is full.

   The glasses on the shelf are empty.

2. The room over the garage is noisy.

   The rooms on the third floor are quiet.

3. The children in the park are healthy.

   The child in the hospital is sick.

4. The dish beside the sink is dirty.

   The dishes in the cupboard are clean.

5. The girls behind the counter are happy.

   The girl at the window is depressed.

6. The student at the desk is hardworking.

   The students around the table are lazy.

7. The windows at the back of the house are open.

   The window on the side of the house is closed.

8. The chair in the corner is comfortable.

   The chairs along the wall are uncomfortable.

9. The woman at the door is elderly.

   The women at the gate are young.

CHART • 5

basic sentences

1. Singular and plural nouns

Series A	Series B
1. This is a shirt.	These are cuff links.
2. This is an album.	These are photos.
3. This is a laptop.	These are flash drives.
4. This is a table.	These are chairs.
5. This is an envelope.	These are stamps.
6. This is a coat.	These are gloves.
7. This is a vase.	These are flowers.
8. This is a pin.	These are pearls.
9. This is a vacuum cleaner.	These are rugs.

2. Possessive forms

Series A	Series B
1. This is Bob's shirt.	These are Tom's cuff links.
2. This is Bill's album.	These are Ken's photos.
3. This is Scott's laptop.	These are Mr. Jones' flash drives.
4. This is Mary's table.	These are Mrs. Smith's chairs.
5. This is Jill's envelope.	These are Peter's stamps.
6. This is Lisa's coat.	These are Karen's gloves.
7. This is Mrs. Ramsey's vase.	These are Mr. Olsen's flowers.
8. This is Emily's pin.	These are Ann's pearls.
9. This is Mrs. Reid's vacuum cleaner.	These are Mrs. Lee's rugs.

CHART • 6 basic sentences

Series A GO + ...ING activities

1. Ron and Steve are going swimming.
2. Janet is going sightseeing.
3. John is going skiing.
4. Mr. and Mrs. Woodhouse are going riding.
5. Ken and Bill are going hiking.
6. Mrs. Andrews and Mary are going shopping.
7. Ryan and Paul are going sailing.
8. Bob and Kyle are going camping.
9. Mr. Miller is going fishing.

Series B GO TO a place + means of transportation

1. Lisa usually takes a bus to school.
2. Mr. Johnson and his family usually walk to church.
3. Ann and Jim usually ride their bikes to the park.
4. George usually takes a taxi home.
5. Chris usually takes the subway downtown.
6. Mr. Andrews usually drives to work.
7. Larry usually takes a ferry to the island.
8. Mr. Oh usually takes a train to Busan.
9. Mrs. Miller and her friend usually fly to New York.

CHART • 7

Two-word verbs: verbal idioms in which a pronoun object comes either before or after the preposition(s)

Series A

1. Mrs. Humphrey put off her dental appointment. She put it off.
2. Mr. Rivers got over his cold. He got over it.
3. Mrs. Harrison got back her money. She got it back.
4. Mrs. Jones tried on the dress. She tried it on.
5. Mr. Black got through with his work. He got through with it.
6. Charles worked out the crossword puzzle. He worked it out.
7. Mrs. O'Brian found out the price. She found it out.
8. Susan got rid of the mistakes. She got rid of them.
9. Mike heated up the room. He heated it up.

Series B

1. Mrs. Humphrey called back the dentist. She called him back.
2. Mr. Rivers gave up ice cream. He gave it up.
3. Mrs. Harrison took back the purchase. She took it back.
4. Mrs. Jones went into the dressing room. She went into it.
5. Mr. Black put away his tools. He put them away.
6. Charles looked up the words in the dictionary. He looked them up.
7. Mrs. O'Brian sent for a catalog. She sent for one.
8. Susan typed the letter over. She typed it over.
9. Mike turned on the heater. He turned it on.

CHART • 8

basic sentences

To contrast countable and uncountable noun usage

1. There are a lot of plates on the table, but only a few cups.
2. There's a lot of computer paper on the shelf, but only a few notebooks.
3. There's a lot of flour in the cupboard, but only a little sugar.
4. There are a lot of shirts on the clothesline, but only a few socks.
5. There are a lot of nails in the bins, but only a little wire.
6. There's a lot of milk in the refrigerator, but only a little fruit.
7. There are a lot of knives in the drawer, but only a few forks.
8. There are a lot of pictures in the room, but only a little furniture.
9. There's a lot of jewelry in the safe, but only a little cash.
10. There are a lot of suits in the store window, but only a few ties.
11. There's a lot of medicine in the first-aid box, but only a few Band-Aids.
12. There's a lot of rice on the plate, but only a little meat.

Two-object verbs: patterns using TO or FOR

1. Simon is offering his seat to an elderly lady.

   He's offering *her his seat.*

2. Mr. Conroy is telling a joke to his boss.

   He's telling *him a joke.*

3. Mrs. Rivers is making sandwiches for the children.

   She's making *them sandwiches.*

4. Philip is buying a present for his mother.

   He's buying *her a present.*

5. Mrs. Hall is paying $50 to the plumber.

   She's paying *him $50.*

6. Adam is writing a postcard to Charlie.

   He's writing *him a postcard.*

7. Scott is getting the mail for his father.

   He's getting *him the mail.*

8. Mr. Collins is leaving a tip for the waiter.

   He's leaving *him a tip.*

9. Timmy is showing his toys to his uncle.

   He's showing *him his toys.*

10. Professor Grant is finding a job for Rich.

    He's finding *him a job.*

11. Mr. Reagan is selling a car to the Johnsons.

    He's selling *them a car.*

12. Mrs. Black is pouring tea for her guests.

    She's pouring *them tea.*

CHART • 10

basic sentences

1. Patterns of comparison

1. John runs faster than Peter.
2. John plays better than Peter.
3. John speaks more fluently than Peter.
4. John works harder than Peter.
5. John drives more carefully than Peter.
6. John sings worse than Peter.
7. John dresses more casually than Peter.
8. John gets up earlier than Peter.

2. Comparing three people

1. John runs faster than Peter,
   but he doesn't run as fast as Paul.
2. John plays better than Peter,
   but he doesn't play as well as Paul.
3. John speaks more fluently than Peter,
   but he doesn't speak as fluently as Paul.
4. John works harder than Peter,
   but he doesn't work as hard as Paul.
5. John drives more carefully than Peter,
   but he doesn't drive as carefully as Paul.
6. John sings worse than Peter,
   but he doesn't sing as badly as Paul.
7. John dresses more casually than Peter,
   but he doesn't dress as casually as Paul.
8. John gets up earlier than Peter,
   but he doesn't get up as early as Paul.

CHART • II

basic sentences

Intransitive verbs and prepositions of motion

1. Look at Luke. He's swimming across the lake.
2. Look at Shawn. He's getting out of the car.
3. Look at Tom. He's climbing up the tree.
4. Look at Mark. He's jumping over the fence.
5. Look at Mrs. Jones. She's rushing into the shelter.
6. Look at Valerie. She's skiing down the hill.
7. Look at Olsen. He's crawling through the bushes.
8. Look at Katie. She's walking under the bridge.
9. Look at the Gregsons. They're driving along the shore.
10. Look at the mailman. He's running away from the dog.
11. Look at Heather. She's riding her bike around the corner.
12. Look at Timmy. He's running toward his mother.

CHART • 12 basic sentences

Transitive verbs of motion

1. The policeman is chasing a man around the corner.
2. Mr. Green is pushing his car toward the garage.
3. The tractor is pulling a car out of the ditch.
4. The man is carrying his wife through the doorway.
5. The cows are following the farmer across the field.
6. Julie is dropping a stone down the well.
7. Jake is kicking the ball into the goal.
8. The boy is throwing the ball to the girl.
9. The boys are throwing snowballs at the man.
10. Mrs. Gregson is lifting the chair over the table.
11. The baby is rolling the toy truck under the sofa.
12. The bulldozer is dragging the logs up the hill.

CHART • 13

basic sentences

The Sunday activities of Mr. Rivers. To practice time clauses with a variety of adverbs: WHILE, DURING, AFTER, etc.

1. He usually reads the newspaper during breakfast.
2. He usually goes to a museum at ten o'clock.
3. He usually mows the lawn when he gets back from the museum.
4. He usually plays tennis while his wife is preparing lunch.
5. He usually takes a shower at 1:15.
6. He usually eats lunch at 1:30.
7. He usually spends time with his family after lunch.
8. He usually helps his wife with the dishes while the children are playing outside.
9. He usually does odd jobs around the house between four and six.
10. He usually changes at 6:45.
11. He usually takes his family out to dinner at 7:00.
12. He usually watches TV while his wife puts the children to bed.

CHART • 14 basic sentences

Patterns of purpose. FOR + noun

1. Go to the barbershop for a haircut.
2. Go to the bakery for some bread.
3. Go to the pool for a swim.
4. Go to the language institute for an English class.
5. Go to the hospital for a checkup.
6. Go to the beach for a vacation.
7. Go to the gas station for some gas.
8. Go to the library for some books.
9. Go to the post office for some stamps.
10. Go to the bank for some money.
11. Go to the coffee shop for a cup of coffee.
12. Go to the tennis club for a game.

CHART • 15

basic sentences

For practice on the preposition BY + ING

1. You can set the alarm clock by turning this knob.
2. You can start the MP3 player by pushing this button.
3. You can focus the camera by turning this ring.
4. You can unlock the door by using this key.
5. You can get to the institute by following this map.
6. You can apply for the job by filling out this form.
7. You can turn on the TV by pushing this button.
8. You can change the channel by using this remote control.
9. You can learn English quickly by following this method.

CHART • 16 basic sentences

BY and WITH used to express instrumentality

1. The applicant filled in the form with a ballpoint pen.
2. The firemen put out the fire with water.
3. The saleswoman wrapped up the purchase with gift wrap.
4. The engineer created the design with a computer.
5. The robber held up the bank with a gun.
6. The gardener pulled up the weeds with his hands.
7. The tailor sewed on the buttons with nylon thread.
8. The terrorists blew up the bridge with a bomb.
9. The accountant added up the figures with a calculator.
10. The waitress wiped off the table with a damp cloth.
11. The lumberjack cut down the tree with an ax.
12. The fashion designer cut out the pattern with a pair of scissors.

CHART • 17

basic sentences

Occupation and corresponding activities

1. Amy Wheeler is a lawyer. She studies patents.
2. Mark Scotti is an executive. He decides company policy.
3. Karen Hyde is a receptionist. She receives visitors and takes phone calls.
4. David Levitzky is on the sales staff. He visits customers.
5. Susan Brady is head of the advertising section. She writes advertising copy.
6. Kevin Bloom is in charge of the training program. He trains new employees.
7. Ben Keenan is an accountant. He goes over the figures.
8. Mary Peterson is a private secretary. She does office work.
9. Jack Martin is a union official. He represents the workers.

CHART • 18

basic sentences

Verb phrases as used in the past tense

1. She put together the sales charts.
2. He did a lot of paperwork.
3. He read a business magazine.
4. They talked with their colleagues.
5. He ordered a new shipment of spare parts.
6. She sent an email.
7. He confirmed his reservation.
8. She checked the tax report.
9. He called the main office.
10. She unpacked her suitcase.
11. He brought the files up to date.
12. They planned new targets.

CHART • 19 basic sentences

More two-word verbs

Series A

1. Samsung opened up new markets. They opened them up.
2. The controller worked on the statistics. She worked on them.
3. The vice-president dealt with foreign clients. He dealt with them.
4. The personnel chief moved on to other work. He moved on to it.
5. Mason Industries kept up with the competition. They kept up with them.
6. LG tried out a new supplier. They tried them out.
7. The executive director cut down on waste. She cut down on it.
8. The financial officer figured out the price. He figured it out.
9. The managing director came up with a plan. He came up with one.

Series B

1. Samsung set up a new branch office. They set one up.
2. The controller opened up a computer spreadsheet. She opened one up.
3. The vice-president took up Spanish. He took it up.
4. The personnel chief handed in the report. He handed it in.
5. Mason Industries came out with a new product. They came out with one.
6. LG used up their stock. They used it up.
7. The executive director called in a consultant. She called one in.
8. The financial officer looked up the exchange rates. He looked them up.
9. The managing director talked over his ideas. He talked them over.

PICTURE • I

basic sentences

Prepositions of location for practice with asking and giving directions from a map

1. This is a map of the downtown area of a small town.
2. Franklin Avenue and Washington Avenue run north and south.
3. The streets run east and west.
4. The river runs from east to west.
5. The train station is south of the river.
6. The library is one block down 11th Street from the church.
7. The park is in the center of town.
8. The river runs through the park.
9. The movie theater is on Franklin Street across from the library.
10. The museum is next to the library.
11. The post office is between the bank and the drugstore.
12. The railroad tracks are behind the office buildings.
13. The shopping center is between 9th and 10th Streets.
14. The apartment buildings are on 10th Street and Washington Avenue.
15. The apartment buildings are along the river.
16. There's a big parking lot beside the shopping center.
17. The gas station is on 9th Street across from the shopping center.
18. The hospital is on the corner of Washington Avenue and 9th Street.
19. The church is next to the school.
20. The hotel is on the other side of the park from City Hall.

PICTURE • 2

basic sentences

To review prepositions of location

1. The desk is in front of the window.
2. There's a pile of books on the desk.
3. There's a dictionary at the bottom of the pile.
4. The dresser is to the right of the desk.
5. The photograph is leaning against the wall.
6. The mirror is over the dresser.
7. The bookcase is in the corner.
8. The bookcase is to the left of the desk.
9. There's a clock on top of the bookcase.
10. The reading lamp is behind the easy chair.
11. The easy chair is between the bed and the dresser.
12. There's a CD player along one wall.
13. The CD cabinet is below the CD player.
14. There's a set of headphones on top of the CD player.
15. There are some pillows on the bed.
16. There's a rug in the middle of the room.
17. The rug is under the easy chair.
18. There's a puppy on the easy chair.
19. There's a cushion on the chair by the desk.
20. There are some CDs on the floor.
21. There are some magazines next to the CDs.
22. There's a big tree outside in the yard.
23. There's a car parked beside the tree.
24. There's a girl sitting in the car.

PICTURE • 3

1. Prepositions of location

1. Mrs. Jill Gregson is in the kitchen.
2. Mr. Bernie Gregson is out in the yard.
3. Cathy Gregson is upstairs in her room.
4. Grandpa Gregson is down in the basement.
5. Joe Gregson is under a tree.
6. Tommy Gregson is in the closet under the stairs.
7. Rachel Gregson is at the side of the house.
8. Grandma Gregson is across the street at a neighbor's house.
9. Little Sue Gregson is in the backyard with her dog.

2. Family relationships

Situation:	*Grandpa Gregson and Grandma Gregson are Bernie's parents. Bernie married Jill and they now have five children: Cathy, Joe, Rachel, Tommy and Little Sue.*
Jill	Jill is Bernie's wife. She is Cathy's, Joe's, etc. mother. She is Mr. and Mrs. Gregson's daughter-in-law.
Bernie	Bernie is Jill's husband. He is Cathy's, Joe's, etc. father. He is Mr. and Mrs. Gregson's son.
Cathy	Cathy is Jill's and Bernie's eldest daughter. She is Joe's, Rachel's, etc. big sister. She is Mr. and Mrs. Gregson's granddaughter.
Joe	Joe is Jill's and Bernie's eldest son. He is Cathy's younger brother. He is Rachel's, Tommy's, etc big brother. He is Mr. and Mrs. Gregson's grandson.

Other relationships:

grandfather	grandmother	grandparents
mother-in-law	father-in-law	"in-laws"
little brother	little sister	
grandchildren		

PICTURE • 4 basic sentences

To give further practice on verbs and prepositions used to express action

1. The bird is flying over the pond.
2. The man is diving into the water.
3. The man is rowing the boat under the bridge.

   Some children are leaning over the bridge.

   One of them is dropping something into the boat.
4. The men in track suits are running around the pond.
5. The little boy is climbing up to the bird's nest.

   The bird is flying around the little boy.
6. The little girl is running away from the angry swan.

   The swan is running after a little boy.
7. The man is chasing the dog across the grass.

   The dog is carrying a drumstick in its mouth.
8. The man is bending over the basket.

   The pickpocket is slipping the wallet out of the man's back pocket.
9. The man is letting the air out of a rubber inner tube.
10. The baby is stepping on the cake.

    His mother is falling over the picnic basket.
11. The camper is crawling out of the tent.
12. The man is throwing a stick toward the pond.

    The dog is running after the stick.
13. The little girl is floating a toy boat on the pond.
14. The little boy is pushing the little girl into the water.

    Her mother is rushing toward them.
15. Some men are dragging a boat out of the water.

    They're dragging it onto the bank.
16. The boy is jumping off the diving board.

17. The man is swimming across the pond.
18. The fisherman is pulling an old boot out of the water.
19. Those boys are throwing stones at a cat.

    The old man is shaking his fist at them.
20. The man with the camera is falling into the pond.
21. The boy is kicking the ball into the pond.
22. Those girls are throwing the ball to each other.

    The ball is going to hit the lady on the head.
23. The boy is dropping a dead fish down the man's shirt.

PICTURE • 5

basic sentences

1. Parts of the body

(A)
1. head
2. hair
3. face
4. forehead
5. eye(s)
6. eyelash(es)
7. eyebrow(s)
8. moustache
9. mouth
10. beard

(B)
11. ear(s)
12. cheek(s)
13. nose
14. lip(s)
15. tongue
16. tooth/teeth
17. jaw
18. chin
19. neck
20. throat

(C)
21. hand(s)
22. palm(s)
23. finger(s)
24. fingernail(s)
25. thumb(s)
26. wrist(s)
27. arm(s)
28. elbow(s)
29. shoulder(s)
30. chest
31. stomach
32. abdomen (belly)

(D)
33. back
34. waist
35. hip(s)
36. leg(s)
37. thigh(s)
38. knee(s)
39. shin(s)
40. calf/calves
41. ankle(s)
42. foot/feet
43. toe(s)
44. heel(s)
45. sole of the foot

(E)
46. a bandage
47. a Band-Aid
48. a scar
49. a cast
50. crutch(es)

2. Expressions for aches, pains, sickness and accidents

(a) The five aches.

1. I have a toothache.
2. You have a headache.
3. He has a stomachache.
4. She has a backache.
5. Do you have an earache?

(b) HURT

I hurt my foot.	My foot hurts.
I hurt my knee.	My knee hurts.
I hurt my wrist.	My wrist hurts.

(c) SORE

My throat is sore.	I have a sore throat.
My back is sore.	I have a sore back.
My eyes are sore.	I have sore eyes. etc.

(d) HAVE A PAIN IN...

I have a pain in my shoulder.

I have a pain in my chest.

I have a pain in my stomach.

(e) BRUISES

He has bruised knees.	He has bruises on his knees.
He has a bruised heel.	He has bruises on his heel.
He has a bruised elbow.	He has bruises on his elbow. etc.

(f) SPRAINS, BREAKS AND FRACTURES

He sprained his ankle.	He has a sprained ankle.
He sprained his wrist.	He has a sprained wrist.
He broke his jaw.	He has a broken jaw.
He broke his leg.	He has a broken leg.
He fractured his rib.	He has a fractured rib. etc.

YOU TOO CAN SPEAK ENGLISH

THE BEST BOOK FOR DEVELOPING YOUR PRONUNCIATION

THE BEST BOOK FOR DEVELOPING YOUR ENGLISH FLUENCY

YOU TOO CAN SPEAK ENGLISH
PRONUNCIATION GUIDE & CHARTS AND PICTURES

2006년 7월 20일 초판 1쇄 발행

편집처 SDA BOOKS
발행인 홍 명 관
인쇄인 신 규 철

발행처 SDA BOOKS
서울특별시 동대문구 청량리동 1번지
전화 (02) 2211-3628
FAX: (02) 2243-3622

인쇄소 시 조 사
서울특별시 동대문구 청량리동 1번지
전 화 (02) 966-0071, 3299-5200

SDA BOOKS